THE CONQUEST OF CANAAN

· The walls of Jericho fall at the blast of trumpets
· The sun and moon halt in their courses at the command of Joshua
· The LORD himself wipes out Israel's enemies with hailstones the size of rocks
· Samson carries the gates of Gaza for forty miles
· Jepthah sacrifices his only daughter because of his triumph
· Moses' grandson becomes an idolatrous priest
· The Benjaminites are destroyed after their rape of a concubine

The books of Joshua and Judges reveal the transition of Israel's history from God's promise to give them Canaan to the reality of facing up to the natives who are determined to keep their land. In this interpretative translation, these books come alive as great ballads of heroes and heroines who fight battles for Israel and God. *The Conquest of Canaan* reveals the innocence and brutality of an age before Israel united under King David and the sublime message of the Jewish prophets took root in the Hebrew soul.

SIDNEY BRICHTO *is a leading Liberal Jewish Rabbi and theologian who writes and lectures on religious and moral issues.*

Also published in *The People's Bible* series:

Genesis
The Books of Samuel
Song of Songs (also including Ruth, Lamentations, Ecclesiastes, Esther)
St Luke & The Apostles

The Genius of Paul (The Apostle's letters)

The People's Bible

The Conquest of Canaan

The Books of Joshua and Judges

newly translated by Sidney Brichto

Sinclair-Stevenson

First published in Great Britain by
Sinclair-Stevenson
3 South Terrace, London SW7 2TB

British Library Cataloguing in Publication Data
A CIP catalogue record for this book is available from
The British Library.

ISBN 0 953 73984 8

Typeset by Rowland Phototypesetting Ltd. Bury St Edmunds, Suffolk.
Printed and bound by Bookmarque Ltd, Croydon, Surrey.

Dedicated to the memory of
GIDEON SCHREIER
26 April 1945 · 12 February 1998

This series of new interpretative translations has been made in memory of my brother, Chanan Herbert Brichto. He loved the Bible with enormous passion not for its historical veracity but for its moral and literary genius. His seminal books Towards a Grammar of Biblical Poetics *and* The Names of God *will, I am convinced, in time revolutionize biblical scholarship. His respect, bordering on worship, of those geniuses who were the vehicles of the 'Still Small Voice of God', is what inspired me to make this attempt to give the Bible back to the people of great, little, or no faith.*

I want to thank Christopher Sinclair-Stevenson whose faith in the project never wavered when my own began to ebb. This attempt is as much his creation as mine. I thank Beverley Taylor, my personal assistant for so many years, for her dedication and help in enabling me to fulfil my creative interests; to Rachel Benjamin for checking the draft of Conquest of Canaan; *and to my wife and children for their advice and patience in my pursuit of this ambitious project.*

SIDNEY BRICHTO

Preface

The simple purpose of this new Bible is to give it back to the people who welcome a good story, fine poetry, and inspiration. For too long now, the Bible has become the best-seller least read. There are several reasons for this, foremost among them the claim of believers that the Bible was written or inspired by God. As our age has become increasingly secular such a claim has turned people away. Also, atheists and humanists maintain that the Bible is a pack of distortions and false prophecies which prevent men and women from accepting their full responsibility for human destiny.

Literate people, however, aware of the Bible as a great classic, feel obligated to read it. Most do not get very far. Repetitions, lack of chronological order, tedious genealogical inserts, stories which cry out for explanations which are not given, incomprehensible thoughts – all these elements, as well as the formal divisions into chapters and verses, have forced most readers to give up even before they have reached the middle of the first book of Genesis.

The purpose of this edition of the Bible is to recast it in such a manner as to make it readable. It will be the complete biblical text faithfully translated after reference to other translations. The biblical narrative style is so sparse that it leaves much to the imagination. This provides a challenge to consider what the author has left out. On occasion, the translator will respond by interacting with the text to fill out the story. To avoid confusion, such elaborations will be indicated by a different print font. This is done with the expectation that some readers will feel that they (and indeed they may be right) could have done better. Such reactions are welcome and proof that the translator's objective of making the Bible come alive has been achieved. Material which appears irrelevant and interrupts the flow is moved into an appendix. Words and sentences will be added, also in a different print font, when necessary to provide continuity and to remove seeming contradictions. References will abound, to enable the reader to find the place in a traditional Bible should he or she wish to make comparisons.

Since the Bible is a library of books, each book or group of books will therefore require special treatment, with a specific introduction to explain how the editor has dealt with the material in his attempt to enable you not only to possess a Bible but to read it with comprehension and pleasure.

The books of Joshua and Judges required radical recasting. My objective of making both books into an easy and continuous read would not have been possible without removing a large chunk from Joshua, namely chapters 12 to 21, to the appendix. Just as the numerous 'begets' have discouraged readers of Genesis, so too would the listing of hundreds of name places to be apportioned to the twelve tribes of Israel, not to mention the allocation of another hundred towns or so to the Levites. It was also necessary to put the first chapter of Judges into the index as it is an addendum to Joshua and repeats almost verbatim two reports found in its preceding book. I have kept to my original intention for the sake of comprehensiveness not to omit any text but to put it into a format which does not inhibit potential readers from enjoying the Bible as literature.

Introduction

That the chosen people, Israel, is portrayed throughout the Hebrew Bible as the most obstinate and unfaithful is not as ironical as one would think. The nation of Israel is a reflection of all the nations of the world – the only difference being that because of the LORD's covenant with Abraham, Isaac and Jacob, Israel became both his ward and representative on earth. Of all the nations, *only* Israel, when she was faithful, worshipped him and *only* she came under his protection.

The books of Joshua and Judges are conclusive proof that Israel was no less brutal than were her neighbours: when Adoni-bezek, the Canaanite warlord is captured, the Israelites cut off his thumbs and big toes. His mournful response was that he had done the same to seventy kings who were forced to collect crumbs under his table. These two books are records of a brutal age in which the deity is as ruthless as the armies of Israel, which he brings to victory or defeat depending on their behaviour towards him.

Joshua and especially Judges should be read as though they were ballads of an age when a few men and women strutted the world stage like mythic heroes and demigods. Enjoying the grace of Yahweh, the LORD, the God of Israel, they have the divine strength to fulfil his will, which is first to conquer the Promised Land and secondly, because of his love for her, to rescue through the appointment of military champions a sinful nation from the oppression of her more powerful neighbours.

The fall of Jericho and Samson and Delilah are among those episodes which have become part of Western legend. Sadly, the pathos of these epic tales, together with others not so well-known, is missed because these books, not being as accessible, *are* hardly ever read. For example, the stoning of a repentant man and his family for taking loot from Jericho, the stratagems of Joshua to bring down the town of Ai, Jael's killing the feared Sisera by hammering a tent peg through his temple into the very ground on which he slept, Samson's brilliant riddles and wordplay as well as his gargantuan strength, Gideon and his reason for dismissing an army of over 30,000 men to rout the enemy with only 300 men, Jepthah's rash vow which costs him the life of his only child – these and others should be read to get a flavour of the biblical age before the centralisation of rule under King Saul and King David.

Some of the material must be of the most ancient to be found in biblical literature. There is a freshness and vitality in the description, dialogue and poetry which reveal the nature of a world in which primitive innocence and 'supernatural' power are the poles of human existence. Occasionally, one is struck by deep emotional sentiment in surprising contrast to the usual calculated exploitation to achieve human as well as divine objectives.

Readers will lose out enormously if, in their interest in Joshua, Ehud, Samson, Gideon, Jepthah, they ignore the most important hero – God. He is a character who weaves in and out of the narrative, sometimes through his messengers but sometimes directly. He has one objective and that is to convince the people of Israel that he is a wonder-working God on whom they are totally dependent for their security and prosperity.

The narrator has the problem of juxtaposing prophetic theology with the reality of Israel's historic situation. This leads to an amazing amount of contradictions in the text, e.g. an enemy town is wiped out and then reappears out of the ashes to oppress Israel. The fact is that, while God promised Israel total subjugation of Canaan after her migration from the Sinai Peninsula, she met with great resistance and many of God's promises were not realised until the establishment of the monarchy. As the LORD's power to do what he wills cannot be questioned, it is necessary either to invent history or to blame the Israelites for his withdrawal from the battle against their enemies. This is a recurring theme throughout the Bible. In the book of Deuteronomy, Israel's waywardness is predicted and cited as the reason for Israel's victimisation at the hands of her enemies.

What is missing from these two books is the moral majesty that is found in parts of the Five Books of Moses and, of course, in the Prophets and Psalms. It is as if the stark reality of Israel's early history is in contradiction to the lofty prophetic sentiments which were the product of a later and more sensitive age. These books, therefore, raise deep and painful theological questions for those religious people who wish to see divine influence and inspiration in all parts of the Bible. But this does make them an even more fascinating read for ordinary readers who have no preconceived ideas as to their divine content. Here, they have a portrayal of powerful men and women of flesh and blood struggling to achieve their objectives of land and sovereignty with the support of the god whom they believe redeemed them from slavery in Egypt. Beyond this, it is an unusual opportunity to seek an understanding of the human mental set of our ancestors who lived some four thousand years ago and who, through their imperfect, primitive but struggling faith, formed the religious and moral foundations of moral civilization.

The Name of God

The name of God as it appears in the Bible is YHVH (Hebrew script has no vowels). This is the ineffable name which was always read as Adonai, meaning 'my Lord'. The traditional translation of YHVH is therefore Lord. The Jerusalem Bible translation refers to God as Yahweh which most scholars believe was the pronunciation of the four consonants. I was tempted to follow this example, because the name makes God into a vital personality – the real hero of *Genesis*: creator, monitor and judge of humanity – rather than an abstract force. Cautious respect for tradition made me hold to 'the Lord', but I hope that the reader will remember that the Lord, the God of Israel, is portrayed as a personality revealing the full range of emotions: paternal justice, maternal compassion, love and reason, regret and anger, punishing and forgiving.

Index of major episodes

Appendix

JOSHUA

JUDGES

The Book of Joshua

THE BOOK OF JOSHUA

After the death of the LORD's servant, Moses, the LORD said to Joshua bin[1] Nun who was Moses' second in command, "Moses my servant is dead. Now, get up to cross the Jordan, to lead this entire people to the land which I am giving to the descendants of Israel. Every place which the sole of your foot touches I have given to you as I promised to Moses, from the wilderness **of Kadesh in the south-east** to the Lebanon **in the north-east**, up to the great river Euphrates which encompasses all the land of the Hittites even to the Great Sea[2] where the sun sets – these will be your borders. No man will be able to withstand your might all the days of your life. As I was with Moses, so will I be with you. I will never fail you or let you down. Be strong and courageous for you will enable this people to possess the land which I promised to give to their ancestors.

"You need only be strong and diligent in obeying all the laws which Moses my servant commanded you. Do not stray from them either to the right or to the left. **Do not do less than he commanded nor more.** If you do this, you will be victorious in all your attempts. Never stop speaking about my book of instructions, reflect upon them day and night so that you diligently obey all that is written there. Only by doing this, will you be successful in your pursuits and triumphant.[3] Have I not ordered you to be strong and courageous? Do not be frightened or anxious for the LORD your God is with you wherever you go."

Joshua immediately gave orders to the commanders of the people: "Go through the entire camp and instruct them with these words, 'Prepare food for yourselves for in three day's time you

---

[1] A Hebrew version of *ben*, meaning 'son of'. It only occurs with Joshua.
[2] The Mediterranean.
[3] An extraordinary concept: military success depends on obedience to God's moral precepts.

will cross the Jordan to take possession of the land which the LORD your God has given you as your inheritance'." **Now the tribes of Reuben and Gad and half of the tribe of Manasseh had decided to settle in Transjordan because they preferred the land there. Moses had agreed on condition that their able-bodied men would cross the Jordan to assist their brothers in conquering the land which the Lord had promised them, after which they could return to their families.**[1]

Joshua spoke to the Reubenites, the Gadites and half of the tribe of Manasseh, "You do remember the orders you received from Moses, the LORD's servant, 'The LORD your God will give you peace and prosperity in this land **you have chosen.**' But on **this condition,** that your wives, your children **under the age of twenty,**[2] your cattle may remain in the land which Moses gave you in Transjordan, but all your warriors will go fully armed alongside your kinsmen to assist them; until the LORD will grant them the same peace and prosperity he has given you. Only when they also take possession of the land which the LORD your God has given them, may you return to the land of your inheritance, to settle in it – for Moses, the LORD's servant, has given it to you in Transjordan, where the sun rises." They answered Joshua **with these words of encouragement,** "All you have said to us we will do. Wherever you send us we will go. Just as we fully obeyed Moses, so will we obey you, so long as the LORD your God is with you as he was with Moses. Whoever **among us** who disobeys your command and does not follow all your instructions will die **as a traitor.** Only be strong and courageous."

---

[1] Numbers 32.
[2] In Numbers 4:29, 31. The Hebrew term for children clearly includes those under twenty. This would make sense because the armies of these tribes could not leave their homes and families totally unprotected.

Two spies are sent to Jericho

Joshua bin Nun secretly despatched two spies from Shittim with these orders, "Go and spy out the land, especially Jericho." Finally they came to the house of a prostitute named Rahab to lodge there, **thinking that the arrival of men at a brothel might go unnoticed.** But the king of Jericho heard that two Israelites had come to spy out the land. He sent instructions to Rahab, "Bring me the men who came to you and entered your home for they have come to spy out the land." The woman, however, had hidden the men. She replied, "These men certainly did come to me but I did not know from where they came. In any event, at the time of the shutting of the gates at nightfall, the men left and I have no idea where they went. Quickly, go after them and you may catch up with them."

She had brought them to her roof where she hid them under the stalks of flax which she had spread out on the roof to dry. The king's men pursued them towards the crossing points of the Jordan River. Immediately after their pursuers had left the city, the gates were locked. Before they fell asleep she came up to them on the roof and said to them, "I know that the LORD has given you this land for our terror of you has overwhelmed us. All who live in the country are melting away before you. We have heard how the LORD dried up the Red Sea for you when you left Egypt and what you did to the two Amorite kings of Transjordan – how you utterly wiped out King Sihon and King Og **and all** their armies. As soon as we heard all this, our hearts melted, neither was there left in any man spirit **to fight against you**, for the LORD your God, he is the God in the heavens above and on the earth below. Now, please swear to me in the name of the LORD that you will be kind to my father's family as I have been kind to you. Give me a guarantee that you will save the lives of my father, mother, brothers and sisters and all that is theirs – save our lives from death!"

The men said to her, "Our lives for yours. If you do not reveal our whereabouts, so it will be, when the LORD gives us this land we will deal kindly and honestly with you." She let them down by a rope through her window because her house was in the city wall and that is where she lived. She said to them, "Run to the hills to avoid your pursuers and hide there for three days until they return. Then you may safely go on your way." The men told her, "We will be innocent of breaking the oath you made us swear to you, unless, when we come into the land, you tie a scarlet ribbon in the window through which you let us down. You must gather into your house your father, mother, brothers and all your father's family. But whoever goes outdoors into the street, his blood is his responsibility, and we are innocent of what happens to him. But for whoever remains with you inside, we will be responsible if anyone harms him. But if you betray us by revealing our whereabouts, we will be released from the oath you made us swear." She replied, "Let it be as you say." She bade them farewell. They set off and she tied a scarlet ribbon in the window.

They reached the hills and stayed there for three days until **they were confident that** their pursuers had returned. The pursuers explored every possible way and byway but could not find them. The two men descended from the hills, crossed the Jordan and came to Joshua bin Nun. They told him all that had happened to them. They concluded their report to Joshua: "The LORD has most certainly put the entire country into our hands because all who live in it are melting away before us."

The Jordan parts for the Israelites

Joshua got up early in the morning and they left Shittim and came to the Jordan, he and the whole people of Israel. They stopped there before crossing it. After three days, the commanders went through the entire camp and ordered the people, "When you see the Ark of the Covenant[1] of the LORD your God carried by the priests the Levites, you will leave your places and follow it. Allow a distance of some two thousand yards between you and it. Do not come close to it but follow it so that you know the direction you must take, for you have never gone this way before."

Joshua instructed the people, "Sanctify yourselves[2] for tomorrow the LORD will perform wonders in your presence." Joshua instructed the priests, "Lift up the Ark of the Covenant and let it pass before the people." They raised the Ark of the Covenant and went before the people. The LORD said to Joshua, "On this day will I exalt you in the sight of all of Israel so that they all know that as I was with Moses, so I am with you. Now, command the priests who carry the Ark of the covenant, 'When you reach the edge of the waters of the Jordan, you shall stop by the Jordan'."

Joshua instructed the Israelites, "Come close so that you may hear the words of the LORD your God." Joshua continued, "By what you are about to see, you shall know that the living God is in your midst. He will without fail drive out from before you the Canaanites, the Hittites, the Hivites, the Perizzites, the Girgashites, the Amorites and the Jebusites. See, the Ark of the Covenant of the master of all the earth will pass before you over the Jordan. Now appoint one man from each of the twelve tribes. When the soles of the feet of the priests who carry the Ark of the LORD, the master of all the earth, touch the waters of the Jordan, the waters shall be cut off – as it flows downstream. The waters of the Jordan shall stand as one large pillar."

[1] Built in the wilderness under Moses' instruction. It contained the two tablets of the law, i.e. the Ten Commandments. It was also called the Ark of Testimony as the Ten Commandments were both the contract of the agreement (covenant) and testimony to the covenant that, if Israel obeyed God's commandments, he would be their eternal protector.
[2] Traditionally understood to mean ritual purification through washing oneself and clothing and avoidance of sexual intercourse.

So it happened, that when the people left their tents to cross the Jordan and the priests were carrying the Ark of the Covenant before them; as the Ark-bearers reached the Jordan, and as the feet of the priests carrying the Ark dipped into the water's edge – for the Jordan overflows all its banks during harvest time – the waters flowing downstream stopped and became higher and higher as one single pillar, a great distance from the city of Adam which is beside Zarethan. So those who went down toward the Sea of the Arabah, even to the Salt Sea, were cut off **from crossing**. But the people of Israel were able to cross right opposite Jericho. The priests who were holding the Ark of the Covenant of the LORD stood firmly on dry ground in the middle of the Jordan. All Israel walked on dry ground until the whole people completed their crossing over the Jordan. **So did the Lord cause the Jordan to dry up before Joshua as he caused the Red Sea to dry up before Moses, his servant. And the people believed in Joshua.**

The twelve stones of testimony

As soon as the entire nation had crossed the Jordan, the LORD spoke to Joshua, "Appoint twelve men from the people, one man from every tribe, and instruct them, 'Take out of the Jordan, from the very place where the priests stood, twelve boulders and carry them to place them where you will stay tonight'." Joshua summoned the twelve men whom he had designated – a man from each tribe, "Go before the Ark of the LORD your God which is in the Jordan and let every man place a boulder on his shoulder according to the number of tribes of Israel. This will be a testimonial for you, so that when your descendants ask you in the future, 'What do these boulders mean to you?' you will say to them, 'Proof that the waters of the Jordan were cut off before the Ark of the Covenant of the LORD. As soon as it went into the river bed, the waters of the Jordan came to a standstill.' These boulders are a memorial to the descendants of Israel forever."

The men of Israel did as Joshua had instructed them. They lifted twelve boulders from out of the Jordan according to the number of tribes of Israel and they carried them to the place they were staying and laid them there. Joshua had another twelve boulders erected in the Jordan itself in the very place where the priests who were holding the Ark of the Covenant stood. They are there to this very day. The priests that bore the Ark stood in the Jordan until Joshua had told the people everything in accordance to Moses' teachings, which God had commanded him to do. Then the people quickly crossed over.

So it was when all the people had crossed over – the Ark of the LORD and the priests proceeding in the sight of the people; the men of Reuben, Gad and half the tribe of Manasseh also fully armed for war crossed over with the Israelites as Moses had instructed them. About forty thousand men armed for war crossed in the presence of the LORD – ready to do battle in the plains of Jericho. On that day, **by these wonders**, did the LORD exalt Joshua before the eyes of all the Israelites. **For this reason**, they stood in awe before him all the years of his life as they had stood in awe of Moses.

Now when the LORD had instructed Joshua, "Tell the priests who carry the Ark of the Testimony to leave the Jordan," Joshua told them, "Come out of the Jordan." As soon as the priests carrying the Ark of the LORD had left the Jordan, at the very moment the soles of their feet touched dry land, the waters of the Jordan returned as before to their natural places and ran over all its banks. The people came out of the Jordan on the tenth day of the first month. They encamped in Gilgal which is on the eastern border of Jericho. The twelve boulders which they took out of the Jordan Joshua erected in Gilgal. He spoke to the people of Israel. "When your descendants ask their fathers, 'What do these stones mean?' they will let their children know, 'Israel came over the Jordan river when it was dry land' for the LORD your God closed up the waters of the Jordan before you until you had crossed over it; so that all the peoples of the earth should know that the LORD's hand is mighty and they may be in awe before the LORD your God forever."

The circumcision of the Israelites

When all the kings of the Amorites that were on the west of the Jordan and all the Canaanite kings who lived by the sea heard how the LORD had dried up the waters of the Jordan before the Israelites until they crossed over, their hearts melted. They were totally demoralised by their fear of the Israelites. At that time the LORD ordered Joshua: "Make yourselves knives from flintstones and organise a further circumcision." Joshua made for himself knives of flintstone and the males of Israel were circumcised at Gibeath-ha-aralot.[1] For this reason Joshua circumcised them: all the males who had come out of Egypt, particularly men of fighting age, had died in the wilderness on the road **to the Promised Land**, after their exodus from Egypt. The males that had come out of Egypt were circumcised; but the males that were born in the wilderness on the way after the Exodus had not been circumcised. The people of Israel had journeyed for forty years in the wilderness until the entire people, particularly the men of fighting age who had come out of Egypt, had died, because they had not listened to the voice of the LORD; **they had not believed that the Lord could bring them safely into the land he had promised to give them.** So the LORD swore that he would not let them see the land which the LORD had sworn to their ancestors that he would give them – a land flowing with milk and honey. He raised up their children in their place **to whom he would fulfil his promise**; Joshua had

[1] Meaning 'Hill of Foreskins'. No such place is known. Exodus 12:37 records the exodus of six hundred thousand besides children. If there was a replacement of only one for one for the generation that died in the wilderness, the task of collective circumcision would have been mammoth. The foreskins could have become a veritable mountain.

them circumcised because they had not been circumcised on their journey. When the entire male population were circumcised, each one of them, they stayed in the camp until they were fully healed.

After the circumcisions, the LORD said to Joshua: "This day I have rolled away the reproach of Egypt from off you, **for in Egypt only their priests and their free men are circumcised. Now you are free and under my rule alone. Your circumcision is the sign of the Covenant between me and you that you will obey me and I will keep you free in the land which I will give to you.** For this reason the name of the place was called Gilgal.[1] The Israelites encamped in Gilgal. They kept the Passover on the evening of the fourteenth day of the month of *Nissan* by the plains of Jericho. They ate of the land's produce on the morning after the Passover, unleavened bread and roasted ears of grain on the same day. Now, the manna[2] **which had been provided by God during their forty years' journey** ceased on the day when they began to eat the land's produce. The Israelites no longer had any manna, but ate from the fruit of the land of Canaan from that year onwards.

Yahweh [The Lord] is a man of war[3]

When Joshua arrived at the outskirts of Jericho, he looked up and suddenly saw a man standing opposite him with a sword

---

[1] Gilgal means circle, but as the Hebrew *gilgal* also means wheel the allusion to 'roll away' is perceived as the basis for its name.

[2] I could not resist quoting the biblical explanation of manna from Alexander Cruden's concordance of the Bible, first published in 1737. "The delicious food wherewith God fed the children of Israel in the deserts of Arabia during their continuance there for forty years. It was a little grain, white like hoar frost, round, and the bigness of coriander-seed. It fell every morning upon the dew, and when the dew was exhaled by the heat of the sun, the manna appeared alone lying upon the rocks or the sand. It fell every day except on the Sabbath and this only about the camp of the Israelites" [Exodus 16: 4–5; 14–15 and Numbers 11:7]

[3] So did Moses' sister Miriam sing after the liberation of the Israelites from Egypt [Exodus 15:3].

drawn in his hand. Joshua approached him with these words, "Are you for us or against us?" He replied, "I am the Captain of the armies of the LORD. I am now come **to give you assistance**." Joshua fell with his face to the ground. He asked, "What has my lord to say to his servant?" The Commander of the LORD's armies said to Joshua: "You need only remove your shoes from your feet for the place where you stand is holy." Joshua did so. And the LORD spoke to Joshua **through the mouth of his Captain**. "Know that I have given into your power Jericho and its king and all its mighty men. All your warriors shall encircle the city once. You will repeat this exercise for six days. Seven priests shall hold seven rams' horns in front of the Ark. On the seventh day you will parade around the city seven times and the priests will keep blowing their horns. Now, when they make a long blast with the rams' horns and you hear its sound, let all your men shout as loudly as they can and the city wall will collapse flat onto the ground. Every warrior will need only cross over from where he stands into the city."[1]

The destruction of Jericho

[Now Jericho was securely closed up out of fear of the people of Israel, none was allowed to leave and no one entered.][2] So did Joshua bin Nun instruct the priests. "Take the Ark of the Covenant and let seven priests carry seven rams' horns before the LORD's Ark." He said to the men, "Go, encircle the city; let all the armed men go before the LORD's Ark." After Joshua gave these instructions, the seven priests holding the seven rams' horns paraded

---

[1] The blasting of the horns and the shouting of some five hundred thousand warriors could create such earth tremors that the walls would be shaken and fall to the ground.

[2] This verse has been transposed from the beginning of chapter 6 for logical consistency.

before the LORD,[1] blowing their horns with the Ark of the Covenant following them. So did the armed soldiers march before the priests who were in the rear behind the Ark blowing the horns without interruption. Joshua commanded his men, "You will not shout, nor let your voices be heard. Let not a word escape from your mouth until the moment I order you to shout. Then you will shout **as you have never shouted before."** So he had the LORD's Ark encircle the city once. Then they returned to the camp where they stayed the night.

Joshua got up early in the morning; the priests took the LORD's Ark. The seven priests holding the rams' horns in front of the LORD's Ark marched without ceasing, blowing on their horns, and **so it was continually**, armed soldiers marching before them and a rear guard behind the LORD's Ark, the priests constantly blowing with horns. **But the soldiers did not utter a sound.** On the second day they also encircled the city once, after which they returned to their camp. This they did for six days. **The people of Jericho were terrified as they heard from the turrets of the city walls the blasting of rams' horns and saw the silent marching of hundreds of thousands of soldiers encircling the city. With each passing day they almost prayed for their inevitable destruction to occur, for the terror was too much for them to bear.**

On the seventh day, they all rose at dawn and encircled the city, but on that day they marched around it seven times. At the end of the seventh circuit, when the priests blew their horns, Joshua called out to the people: "Shout, for the LORD has granted you the city. The city is dedicated to the LORD **and under an interdict, nothing shall be taken as spoil, nothing shall live**, except Rahab the prostitute – she shall live and all who are with her in her home because she hid the messengers whom we sent. Be careful, stay away from all that is under interdict, lest you be

---

[1] Is the LORD before whom they paraded personified by the Captain of his armies who spoke to Joshua?

cursed by taking anything under the interdict and cause the camp of Israel to be cursed, thus causing great distress. However, all silver and gold and brass and iron vessels are dedicated to the LORD. They will become part of the LORD's treasury, **for they are his spoils as the victory is his.**"

The men shouted and the priests blew their horns. And, when the men heard the sounds of the horns, they shouted with an even mightier shout, so that the **earth shook and the** walls fell down flat **before them**, so that the men could go straight into the city, every man going straight into it. So did they capture the city. They destroyed everything in the city with the sword – men and women, young and old, oxen, sheep and donkeys.[1] Joshua said to the two men who spied out the land, "Go into the prostitute's house and bring out the woman and all that she has, **her family and possessions** as you swore to her." The young men who were the spies went into her house, **which was the only part of the wall which remained standing,** to bring out Rahab, her father and mother, her brothers and all she had and all her kinsmen. They put them outside the encampment of Israel. They then burnt the city with everything in it, except for the gold, silver and the brass and iron vessels which they placed in the treasury of the house of the LORD.[2] But Rahab the prostitute, and her father's household and all that was hers, Joshua kept alive and she lived among the Israelites and her descendants until this

---

[1] This tale was told in a primitive and brutal period. It is incomprehensible to a modern civilised person that there should appear to the narrator no problem for a moral and compassionate God who asks his people to love their neighbours as themselves, even when these neighbours are enemies, and should permit the wholesale slaughter of a foreign but indigenous people. This is proof that, at the time of this narrative, the LORD was perceived to be the God of Israel without any concern for people worshipping other gods. A modern parallel to make us feel less self-righteous is the fact that Western governments will provide social welfare for their own citizens while at the same time sell arms to feed civil wars and destruction abroad.

[2] A shrine yet to be established.

very day because she hid the messengers whom Joshua sent to spy out Jericho.[1]

Joshua made an oath before the people at that time, "Cursed by the LORD be the man who stands up to rebuild this city of Jericho. He who lays its foundation will lose his first-born and his youngest when he puts up its gates." Thus was the LORD with Joshua. His fame spread throughout the land.

The Israelites run for their lives

The people of Israel, however, violated the interdict: for Achan ben Carmi ben Zabdi ben Zerah of the tribe of Judah took spoil from the city. The LORD's anger flared up against the people of Israel. It was at the time that Joshua sent men from Jericho to Ai, which is by Beth-aven east of Beth-el, with these instructions, "Go and spy out the land." The men went to spy out Ai. They returned to Joshua with this report, "It is not necessary for all our forces to go up. Two or three thousand will be sufficient to go and defeat the men of Ai for they are few in number. Do not trouble the entire fighting force to go there." So three thousand men went up but fled before the men of Ai. The men of Ai killed some thirty-six Israelites and pursued them from their gates until they had crushed them. They struck out at them as they went down **to return to their camp. Now** the hearts of the Israelites melted and became as water.

Not understanding the cause of this defeat, Joshua tore his clothes and fell prostrate on the ground before the LORD's Ark until evening. Not only he but the elders of Israel put dust on their hair **as a sign of mourning.** Joshua cried, "Woe, my LORD, God, why did you make such efforts to bring this people over the

[1] The generosity towards Rahab, whose only interest was to save her own skin, is in stark contrast to the Israelite annihilation of Jericho. According to one Rabbinic tradition, Joshua married her and she was the ancestress of Jeremiah.

Jordan to hand them over to the Amorites to destroy us? We would have been happy to remain in Transjordan. My LORD, what can I say now that Israel has turned her back in flight before her enemies? When the Canaanites and all who live in the land hear of what happened, they will surround us and cut off all memory of us from the earth, and what will you do to redeem your great reputation **as a god of deliverance?**"

The LORD spoke **angrily** to Joshua, "Get up, why have you fallen on your face? Israel has sinned. They have even broken **the conditions of** my covenant which I commanded them. They broke the interdict. They stole and acted fraudulently – they have put the stolen items among their own things.[1] Therefore the descendants of Israel will not stand up against their enemies. They had to turn their backs in flight before their enemies because they are accursed. I will not be with you again until you destroy the accursed among you. Go! Sanctify the people! Give them this command, 'Sanctify yourselves for tomorrow, for thus says the LORD, the God of Israel. There is a curse among you, O Israel; you will not be able to stand up before your enemies until you remove the accursed thing from among you. In the morning you shall approach **the Lord** tribe by tribe. The tribe found guilty by the LORD shall then approach clan by clan. The clan found guilty by the LORD shall approach family by family. The family found guilty shall approach man by man. He who has violated the ban will be burnt with fire, he and all that is his, because he has broken the covenant of the LORD and because he committed an abomination in Israel'."

---

[1] Collective responsibility reflects Biblical morality. Achan alone was guilty. Yet, due to his offence, the Israelite troops are routed with thirty-six dead.

Achan and his children are stoned

Joshua got up early the next morning and had the tribes of Israel approach the Lord.[1] Judah was singled out, then the clan of the Zerahites, then the family of Zabdi, then Achan ben Carmi ben Zabdi ben Zerah of the tribe of Judah was identified. Joshua said to Achan, "My son, I beg of you, glorify the Lord, the God of Israel by confessing before him. Tell me what you have done. Do not conceal anything from me." Achan replied to Joshua, "I have most certainly sinned against the Lord, God of Israel. This is what I have done. When I saw among the spoils a scarf from Shinar and two hundred shekels of silver and a brick of gold weighing fifty shekels I lusted after them and took them. They are hidden underground in my tent with the silver at the bottom." Joshua sent a few men who ran into his tent and it was hidden there with the silver at the bottom **of the spoil**. They took the booty out of the tent and brought it before Joshua and the community of Israel and laid it down before the Lord.

Joshua together with all the Israelites took Achan the descendant of Zerah, the silver, the scarf, the brick of gold and his sons and daughters, his oxen, donkeys and sheep, his tent and all that he owned. They brought them up into the Valley of Achor. Joshua admonished him, "Why have you caused us such trouble? **Because of your sin, thirty-six men of Israel were killed and we and our God were ashamed before our enemies.** Now, the Lord will trouble you today!" Then all the Israelites stoned him to death and they burnt them with fire after stoning them to death.[2]

---

[1] What is the narrator suggesting? How were they brought before the Lord? Was it before the Ark of the Covenant? Was the guilty party determined by sacred lots? The description may be vague because the author was uncertain himself.

[2] The severity of the punishment is barbaric, especially in the view of the Mosaic law which forbade the execution of children for their father's sin [Deuteronomy 24:16]. Of course, Deuteronomy may have been written after Joshua (though it precedes it in the Bible) and may reflect a more civilised morality. In early biblical times, a man was seen to live through his children.

They piled a great heap of stones over him, which is there even now. The LORD's fierce anger was abated. For this reason that place is still called the Valley of Trouble.

The battle for the City of Ai

The LORD encouraged Joshua, "Do not be afraid or anxious. Summon all your warriors and go up to Ai. See, I have given the king of Ai, his people, city and land into your hand. You will do to Ai and to her king what you did to Jericho and her king. This time you may keep the spoil and cattle for yourselves. Prepare to ambush the city dwellers by encamping behind it **on its western side.**"

So Joshua with all his warriors advanced towards Ai. He picked thirty thousand of his most valiant men to send them out during the night with these instructions: "You will lie in ambush behind the city. Do not go far from the city and be ready for action. I and all those remaining with me will advance towards the city **gates.** Now, when they come out against us **as they did before,** we will flee from them. They will pursue us **and we will run** until we have drawn them away from the city, for they will think, 'They are once again fleeing from us as they did before.' We will continue to flee from them. Then you will ambush the city and capture it. The LORD will place it into your hands **because all its soldiers will be running after us.** When you have captured the city, put the city into flames. I order you to do what the LORD has commanded."[2]

Thus only by killing them did one really destroy the guilty man. In light of this view, it is significant that Achan's wife is not mentioned. She was not stoned perhaps because she was the daughter, i.e. the posterity, of another man. The violence of the Israelites can be explained by the consequences of Achan's crime. The fact that we are told that God was appeased by Israel's behaviour reveals a primitive concept of the deity.

[2] Unlike on the previous occasion, Joshua does not underestimate the enemy. Though God is on his side, the battle against Ai will be won through a wily strategy which takes advantage of Israel's previous defeat. Perhaps it was

Joshua sent them off. They arrived at the place where they were to conceal themselves in readiness for the ambush, which was between Beth-el and Ai, on the western side of Ai. But Joshua slept that night with his army. He got up early in the morning and mustered the army. He and the elders led the warriors to Ai. All the men of war who were with him went up towards the city and encamped on the north side of Ai. Now there was a valley between them and the city of Ai. He then despatched some five thousand men with instructions to conceal themselves in readiness for an ambush between Beth-el and Ai, on the west side of Ai. So the army put on their battle array – all those who were at the north of the city and those lying in wait at the west of the city. Joshua went that night with the remaining forces into the middle of the valley.

When the king of Ai saw **Joshua and his forces in the valley**, the men of the city quickly woke up early in the morning and went out to attack Israel. At the agreed time, he and his army went to the plain at the top of the valley. He was, of course, unaware of the ambush behind the city. Joshua and all the Israelite troops pretended to be beaten back by them. They began to run away towards the wilderness. **Smelling a great victory**, they summoned all the men who were still in the city to join in pursuit. They ran after Joshua until they were drawn away from the city. There did not remain one able-bodied man in either Ai or Beth-el who did not go in pursuit of the Israelites. The city was left wide open and undefended.

The LORD said to Joshua, "Stretch out your javelin towards Ai, and I will give it into your hand." So Joshua stretched out his javelin in the direction of the city. The men in ambush quickly left their places. At the moment Joshua stretched forth his javelin towards

Israel's complacency and not Achan's crime which was the cause for her earlier setback. Biblical history, however, must see God's hand in everything.

the city, they stormed into it. They seized it and immediately set fire to it. When the men of Ai looked behind them, they saw smoke rising towards the skies from their city. They could not run away because the Israelites who had been fleeing to the wilderness turned to confront their pursuers. When Joshua and the Israelites saw that the ambush against the city had succeeded, as smoke was rising from the city, they turned round and killed the men of Ai. When they, **the Israelites**, left the city which was ablaze to attack them, they, **the men of Ai,** were surrounded by the Israelites on all sides. They slaughtered them . They allowed no one to escape. But the king of Ai they took alive, and brought him to Joshua.

When the Israelites had finished killing all the men of Ai on the battlefield, and in the wilderness where they had pursued them – and all had fallen by the sword – Israel returned to the city of Ai and put it to the sword. All those that fell that day were twelve thousand men and women – all the inhabitants of Ai. Joshua had kept his arm outstretched with his javelin until he had completely destroyed all of the city's inhabitants. Only the cattle and the plunder of the city did the Israelites take as spoil, according to what the LORD had agreed with Joshua. So did Joshua burn down Ai and make it into a pile of ruins, totally desolate, as it is today. He hanged the king of Ai on a tree until evening. When the sun was going down, Joshua ordered his body to be taken down and left by the entrance of the city gate. They threw over him a great mound of stones which is there to this very day.

Then Joshua built an altar to the LORD God of Israel in Mount Ebal. As Moses, the LORD's servant, had commanded the people of Israel, as it is written in the Scroll of the Laws of Moses, it was an altar of unhewn stones, on which no one had used an iron tool.[1] They offered on it burnt offerings to the LORD and also

---

[1] The traditional reasoning for the absence of iron tools is that iron was used for war and therefore should not desecrate the altar of the LORD which was designed to create peace and harmony between man and God.

sacrificed offerings of peace.[1] On the stones of that place, Joshua inscribed a copy of the Laws of Moses. He wrote this in the presence of the Israelites. All the Israelites and their elders and their magistrates stood on both sides of the Ark and before the priests the Levites who carried the Ark of the Covenant of the LORD – strangers as well as citizens participated. Half of them stood facing Mount Gerizim and half of them facing Mount Ebal, as Moses had commanded them in the past as to how they should bless the people of Israel.

Afterwards, he read all the words of the Law, **including** the blessings and the curses **which would be rewards for those who obeyed and punishments for those who did not** – all that which was written in the Scroll of the Law. Not a word of all that Moses commanded did Joshua fail to read out before the entire congregation of Israel, including women, children and the strangers who were among them.[2]

The treaty with the Gibeonites

Now, when all the kings that were west of the Jordan, in the hill-country and in the lowlands and along the entire coast of the Great Sea before Lebanon – the kings of the Hittites, the Perizzites, the Hivites and the Jebusites – heard of what had hap-

---

[1] The burnt offerings were total offerings to God. The peace offerings were eaten by those who made the sacrifice – only the animal fat was burnt as an offering to God.

[2] It is significant that all those non-Israelites who fled from Egypt were given the same rights and privileges as the Israelites because they had come under God's protection as they obeyed his laws. Those outside the Covenant such as the people of Jericho and Ai were the people whose sins justified God taking their land to give to the Israelites which he had promised to Abraham. The reason given for the four hundred years the Israelites spent in Egypt was to give the Amorites who lived in Canaan the opportunity to be sufficiently sinful to deserve their destruction. "And they shall come back here in the fourth generation, for the iniquity of the Amorites is not yet complete." [Genesis 15:15]

pened to the city of Jericho and Ai, they united to fight against Joshua and Israel as one army.

When the inhabitants of Gibeon, however, heard how Joshua had dealt with Jericho and Ai, they devised a clever stratagem. They went in the disguise of ambassadors who had come a long way. They put old sacks on their donkeys and wine-skins which were faulty with patches sewn over the cracks. Their sandals were worn out and patched as was their clothing. The bread in their provisions was dry and broken into pieces. They came to Joshua's camp at Gilgal and said to him and the Israelites, "We have come from a far country. Now, therefore, make a pact with us." The men of Israel replied to the Hivites, "Perhaps you live in the vicinity. If this is so we cannot make a treaty with you for our God has commanded us not to make any treaties with the peoples of this land. Moses said to us, 'You must utterly destroy them, grant them no terms and show them no mercy'."[1]

They said to Joshua, "We are your servants and at your mercy." He asked them, "Who are you and where do you come from?" They answered him, "From a very distant country have your servants come because of the reputation of the LORD your God. His fame has spread because of all that he did in Egypt and all that he did to the two kings of the Amorites east of the Jordan, to Sihon, the king of Heshbon and Og, the king of Bashan who was at Ashtaroth. For this reason, our elders and the inhabitants of our land instructed us, 'Take for yourselves sufficient provisions for the journey and go to meet the Israelites and acknowledge that we are your servants: now make a treaty of peace with us.'

---

[1] Deuteronomy 7:2–4. The command continues, "you shall not intermarry with them . . . for they will turn your children away from me to worship other gods and the LORD's anger will burn against you and he will immediately destroy you!" The fear that the Israelites would be corrupted by the pagan peoples is the rationale given for their barbarisms. Ironically, in the end, Joshua did not succeed in destroying all the peoples and indeed the tribes of Israel did turn to worshipping the local gods.

See our bread which was hot when we took it as our provision from our homes on the day we left to go to you – now it is dry and falling to pieces. These wine-skins which we filled were new and now they are cracked. These, our clothes and sandals are worn out because of the very long journey." The Israelites took their provisions **to see if it was as they said. When they saw that it was dry, they believed them** and did not consult the mouth of the LORD. So Joshua made peace with them and a covenant with them, to preserve their lives – so did the heads of the community swear to them.

Three days after they made the pact with them, they heard that they were their neighbours and that they were living close by. The people of Israel set off and arrived at their towns on the third day. The towns were Gibeon, Chephira, Beeroth and Kiriath-yearim. But the people of Israel did not attack them because the heads of the community had sworn to them by the LORD, the God of Israel. The entire community protested to their chiefs. But they spoke to the whole community, "We have sworn to them by the LORD the God of Israel. Now, therefore, in no way can we harm them. This is what we will do to them. We will let them live. Otherwise, the wrath **of the Lord** will be on us because of the oath we swore to them, **but we will make them our servants.**" So the chiefs made this order about them, "Let them live." So they became servants for the Israelites – hewers of wood and drawers of water for all the members of the community, as the chiefs had commanded.

Then Joshua summoned them:

– "Why have you deceived us by telling us, 'We are very far from you when you live among us? Now, therefore, you are cursed. You will always provide us with slaves, both hewers of wood and drawers of water for the house of my God."
– "**We did this** because your servants were very clearly told that the LORD your God commanded his servant Moses, that when

he gave you all this land, you had to destroy all the inhabitants in your approach. It is because we were so terrified for our lives that we did this. But now, we are at your mercy. Whatever seems right to you – do to us."

So did Joshua act towards them; he spared them from the might of the Israelites and they did not attack them. But on that day Joshua assigned them as hewers of wood and drawers of water **which they are** until this very day for the whole community and for the altar of the LORD, in the place of his choosing.[1]

The sun stands still for Joshua

Adoni-zedek king of Jerusalem heard that Joshua had taken Ai and had destroyed it and had dealt with Ai and her king as he had dealt with Jericho and her king. When he also heard that the Gibeonites had made a peace treaty with Israel, even though they lived among the Israelites, they, **Adoni-zedek and the neighbouring kings,** were extremely anxious because Gibeon was as large as the royal cities. In fact it was larger than the city of Ai and had a sizeable army. **Adoni-zedek thought, "If the Gibeonites are allowed to break ranks and make peace with Israel, there will be no hope for me and my fellow kings to withstand Joshua and his people. We must destroy them as an example to others who would make peace with the Israelites."**

Adoni-zedek king of Jerusalem therefore sent this message to Hoham king of Hebron and Piram king of Jarmuth and Japhia king of Lachish and to Debir king of Eglon, "Come up to assist me in attacking Gibeon for she has made a treaty of peace with

---

[1] This punishment must have been a face-saving device for Joshua and the Israelite chiefs. It was totally impractical as the Gibeonites, etc. would need to sustain themselves and not be a burden upon the Israelites. Possibly, as a token of their subservience, a number of them might have been delegated for menial tasks in the Temple.

Joshua and the people of Israel." So did the five kings of the Amorites muster their armies to encamp before Gibeon to attack her. The men of Gibeon sent a message to Joshua who was camping in Gilgal: "Do not fail your servants, but come quickly to save us. Help us, for all the Amorite kings who live in the hill-country have joined together to attack us." Joshua went up from Gilgal, with his full army – all his most experienced warriors.

The LORD reassured Joshua, "You need not fear them because I have put them into your hands. Not one of them will be able to stand up against you." Joshua took them by surprise, for they had marched from Gilgal through the night. The LORD confounded them before Israel. They inflicted upon them a great slaughter at Gibeon. They pursued them by the road which goes up to Beth-horon – killing them all the way to Azekah and Makkeda. **Not only this,** but as they ran away from the Israelites at the point of the descent from Beth-horon, the LORD hurled upon them great hailstones from heaven as they fled to Azekah and they died. More died from the hailstones than those killed by the swords of the Israelites.[1]

Joshua then petitioned the LORD on that day when he delivered the Amorites into the hands of the people of Israel. He shouted before all the Israelites:

"Sun – stand still over Gibeon

Moon – stand still over the valley of Aijalon."

The sun stood still and the moon stopped until our nation had executed vengeance over their enemies. Is this not written down in the scroll of Jashar,[2] that the sun stopped in the middle of the

[1] The reader should note how careful the narrator is in giving credit for all of Israel's victories to the LORD, God of Israel, even to the point of intervening with all the power at his command. Hailstones large enough to kill were as unlikely an occurrence in the Promised Land as was the sun (or earth) standing still at the command of Joshua.

[2] This book has disappeared. 'Jashar' means righteous or upright. It may have been annals of Israelite heroes and heroines. It is referred to in II Samuel 1:18.

25

heavens and did not set for an entire day, **so that the Israelites
could see their enemies in order to destroy them.** Never was there
a day like that before or afterwards, when the LORD obeyed the
command of a man, because the LORD was fighting for Israel.[1]

The five kings fled and hid in a cave in Makkedah.[2] When
Joshua was informed: "We have found the five kings hiding in a
cave in Makkedah," he gave these instructions, "Roll into the
cave's opening great boulders and place men by it to keep guard.
You others do not stop, **even though with their kings as captives
the war is won,** but press on after your enemies and strike them
on their rearguard. Do not allow them to reach into their **fortified**
cities, for the LORD your God has delivered them into your hands."
When Joshua and the men of Israel had finished inflicting upon
them a great massacre, until they were wiped out with only a
remnant escaping to their fortified cities, the whole army returned
intact to Joshua's camp at Makkedah. There was none left even
to snarl against the Israelites, **still less to fight against them.**

Joshua said, "Open the cave entrance and bring me the five
kings." They did this. The five kings of Jerusalem, Hebron, Jarmuth,
Lachish and Eglon were brought to him. When the kings were
brought to Joshua, he summoned all the men of Israel and said to
the commanders of his army, "Come closer and put your feet on
the necks of these kings." They approached and put their feet on
their necks. Then Joshua said to them, "You need not be afraid or
anxious, but be strong and confident, for just **as he has dealt with
these men,** so will the LORD deal with all your enemies against
whom you wage war." After this, Joshua struck and killed them and
hung them on five trees where they hung until nightfall. At sun set,
he ordered that they be taken down from the trees and thrown into

---

[1] I have omitted 10:15 because the verse is misplaced. It reappears again as
verse 43.
[2] This must be literary licence. One would have expected the five kings each to
be leading his own army and not to be together. It is a fable: as they conspired
together, so must they die together.

the cave which was their hiding place, and to lay large boulders at the entrance to the cave. **There they are** until this very day.

Joshua conquered Makkedah on that day. He put to the sword its king and everyone who lived there. No one survived. He treated the king of Makkedah as he had the king of Jericho. Then Joshua moved from Makkedah with the Israelite army to Libnah and attacked it. The LORD delivered it with its king into the hands of Israel. They put it and all the people in it to the sword – no one escaped. He dealt with its king just as he had done to the king of Jericho. Then he moved on to Lachish with all his forces, encamped there and attacked the city **Once again** the LORD delivered Lachish into the hand of Israel and Joshua conquered it on the second day. He put it to the sword – every person there, just as he had done to Libnah. When Horam king of Gezer came up to help Lachish, Joshua defeated him and his army until not one soldier was left alive.

Joshua moved on from Lachish with all his forces to Eglon where they encamped and attacked it. They conquered it on the same day and destroyed it with the sword – he wiped out everyone who lived there just as he had done in Lachish. Joshua then moved from Eglon with his forces to Hebron. They attacked and conquered it, destroying it with the sword – its king,[1] all the villages roundabout and every person who lived there. He left no one alive just as he had done in Eglon. He destroyed it and everyone of its inhabitants.

Joshua then turned back with all his forces to Debir which they attacked. He conquered it, its king and all the villages around it. He put them all to the sword and wiped out every person in the area. He left no one alive. As he had done to Hebron, so did he do to Debir and its king and as he had also done to Libnah and

---

[1] As Joshua had already killed the king of Hebron, who was among the confederation of the five kings, this is an anomaly unless we assume that it was his successor.

its king. So did Joshua destroy the entire area: the hill-country, the South, the Shephelah [lowlands] and the slopes with all their kings. He left no one alive – he annihilated everything that breathed as the LORD, God of Israel commanded. So did Joshua attack them all from Kadesh-barnea even up to Gaza and the district of Goshen up to Gibeon. All the kings and their lands did Joshua conquer in one fell swoop – but only because the LORD, God of Israel fought on Israel's side. Only then did Joshua with all the Israelites return to their camp in Gilgal.

Israel's onslaught continues

When Jabin king of Hazor heard **of the great victories of Joshua over the Amorite kings and how the Israelites had devastated the cities of the south,** he joined a confederation with Jobab king of Madon and the kings of Shimron and Achshaph and the other kings that ruled over the north – in the hill-country, in the Arabah [Jordan valley] south of Chinnereth, in the lowlands and in the district of Dor on the west – the entire area including the Canaanites who lived in the east and west, the Amorites, Hittites, Perizzites and Jebusites who lived in the hill-country and the Hivites who lived below Hermon in the district of Mizpah. These kings went out to battle with all their armies – a great multitude as numerous as the sands of the seashore and with myriad horses and chariots. All these kings met together and pitched their camps together by the waters of Merom to do battle against Israel.

The LORD encouraged Joshua, "You need not be frightened of them for at this time tomorrow I will deliver all of them as dead men before the Israelites. You will then hamstring their horses and burn their chariots to cinders."[1] Joshua and all his warriors

---

[1] The order not to take the horses or chariots as spoil for their own use is one more indication that the Israelites needed nothing but God's support to win their battles. The verse in Psalms, 'Salvation belongs to the LORD' [3:9] was understood militarily as well as spiritually.

made a surprise attack on them by the waters of Merom. The
LORD delivered them into the hands of the Israelites. They struck
them down and chased them as far as Great Zidon and Misre-
photh-maim [near Tyre] and the valley of Mizpeh in the east. They
slaughtered them so that none remained alive. Joshua obeyed the
LORD's instructions, he cut the tendons of the horses' hind
legs so that they would be useless for battle and burnt their
chariots.

Then Joshua turned back to conquer Hazor, to put her king to
the sword. Previously Hazor had been pre-eminent among all
those kingdoms. Joshua put all the people in it to the sword –
destroying them completely, not a person survived. Then he had
Hazor burnt down.[1] All the kings and their cities did Joshua
conquer, attacking them and utterly destroying them as Moses,
the LORD's servant, had commanded them **in the wilderness.** The
cities that were built on high places he did not burn **for they
would be for the Israelites to settle.** Only Hazor did Joshua burn.
The Israelites plundered the cities of all their spoils, but put every
man to the sword until they were all destroyed, leaving no one
that had the breath of life in him. This was as the LORD had
commanded Moses his servant, so did Moses instruct Joshua to
do and so he did. He left not a thing undone of all that the LORD
had instructed Moses.

So did Joshua conquer all this land: the hill-country, the whole
Negev [south], the whole area of Goshen and the Shephelah [the
lowlands], and the Arabah [the Jordan valley] and the hill-
country of Israel and its lowlands, from the smooth mountain
that goes toward Seir and up to Baal-gad in the valley of Lebanon
below Mount Hermon. He conquered all their kings, attacked
them and put them to death. Joshua warred with these kings for

---

[1] This tale of utter destruction is in the world of fantasy. Not that long after
Joshua's conquest we are informed that Jabin the king of Hazor oppressed the
Israelites for twenty years [Judges 4:3] see p. 47.

a very long time.[1] There was no city which made peace with the people of Israel except for that of the Hivites who inhabited Gibeon. Every other city they conquered because it was the LORD's intention to make their enemies stubborn and take the Israelites on in battle to justify their utter destruction, so that they would find no favour with the Israelites and be destroyed as the LORD had ordered Moses.[2]

During that period he destroyed the Anakim[3] [the giants] who lived in the hill country, from the cities of Hebron, Debir and Anab and from all the hill country **which now belongs to the tribe** of Judah and the hill country **which now is settled** by **the ten tribes of** Israel. Joshua wiped them out together with the towns they occupied. Not one of the Anakim was left alive, except in the Philistine cities of Gaza, Gath and Ashdod where some did remain. So Joshua conquered the whole country as the LORD had promised Moses. Joshua gave it as an inheritance to Israel, dividing it among all the tribes. And the land had rest from war.[4]

---

[1] The impression given to us, however, is that he wiped out all his enemies within months. With the LORD on his side, they appeared to fall before Joshua like flies. This verse may be the return of the narrator to reality.

[2] The impression given here is that the Israelites must have had a more lenient policy towards the natives had they sued for peace. This puts the full responsibility for the annihilation of the populace on God – a far cry from the God of Abraham who accepts his reprimand for being prepared to punish the innocent with the wicked at the destruction of Sodom. [Genesis 18].

[3] The Anakim who were descendants of the Nephilim – the sons of the divine beings who slept with the women of the earth [see Genesis 6:4]. It was their stature which terrified the men that Moses sent to spy out the Promised Land. They came back with the report that they never would be able to conquer the country. Because of this lack of faith in God, that whole generation was doomed to die in the wilderness, with the exception of Caleb and Joshua, the spies who believed in God's power to deliver. [Numbers 13:31–33; 14:20–24]. This indicates the mythological elements of this historical narrative. Some such as Goliath were kept alive to challenge David and other heroes.

[4] That they did not conquer the entire land is seen in subsequent narrative material especially Chapters 12 to 21, which summarise the conquests of Joshua and the division of the land between the twelve tribes and the apportionment of cities of the Levites and the Cities of Refuge. These are in the appendix for the interested reader.

The tribes of Reuben, Gad and half of the tribe of Manasseh are given leave to return home to trans-Jordan

So Joshua summoned the Reubenites, the Gadites and half the tribe of Manasseh. Joshua praised them, "You have been obedient to that which Moses the LORD's servant commanded you and you have also obeyed all my orders. You have not forsaken your kinsmen all these days **but have fought on their behalf to conquer the land which will be their inheritance.** Until now you have obeyed the LORD your God by abiding by his charge **to support your kinsmen.** And, now that the LORD your God has given the security of peace to your kinsmen as he promised them, you are able to return to your homes, to the land of your settlements which Moses the servant of the LORD gave to you on the other side of the Jordan. Only remember to be very careful to obey the commandments and teachings which Moses the LORD's servant taught you – to love the LORD your God, to walk in all his ways, to keep and hold fast to all his commandments and to serve him with all your heart and soul." So did Joshua bless them and send them on their way. And they readied themselves for their return home.

This is what happened. As you know, to one half of the tribe of Manasseh Moses had given possession of land in Bashan, **on the other** side of the Jordan. To the other half of the tribe Joshua gave land among their brother-tribes on the west side of the Jordan. Also, when Joshua sent them home, he blessed them by telling them, "Take with you on your return as much wealth as you can – herds of cattle, silver, gold, brass and iron and lots of clothing. Divide the spoil of your enemies together with your kinsmen **who stayed behind to protect the women and children.**" The men of Reuben and the men of Gad and the half tribe of Manasseh proceeded to return. They left the people of Israel at

Shiloh [in the land of Canaan] – the resting place of the LORD's Ark – to go to the district of Gilead in the place of their settlement which had been granted to them according to the LORD's command given to Moses.

When they reached the region before the Jordan river, but still in the land of Canaan, the men of Reuben, Gad and half of the tribe of Manasseh built an altar by the Jordan. It was an altar of great size to impress its viewers. When the people of Israel heard that the men of Reuben and Gad and half of Manasseh had built an imposing altar on the border of Canaan right by the Jordan on the side that belongs to the **other** tribes of Israel, they said, **"Who gave them the authority to build an altar on land not theirs and to offer sacrifices there?"** When the news reached all the tribes of Israel, the whole confederation of the people of Israel mustered themselves together at Shiloh to attack them.

But first the people of Israel sent emissaries to Reuben, to Gad and to the half-tribe of Manasseh in the land of Gilead. Leading them was Phinehas the son of Eleazar the priest, and the delegation consisted of ten chiefs, one chief of a clan representing each of the tribes of Israel. Each one of them was the head of a most important clan of Israel. They came to Reuben, Gad and the half-tribe of Manasseh in the land of Gilead and remonstrated with them, "So says the entire community of the LORD: What is the reason for this treachery by which you have betrayed the God of Israel, to turn away from the LORD on this day, by building an altar for yourselves? In this you have rebelled against the LORD. Is it not enough that we were sinful at Peor **when we participated in sacrifices to the god of the Moabites?** We are still not cleansed from that offence even until this day, even though a great plague came upon the LORD's community **because of it.** Will you then this day turn away from following the LORD? And, if you rebel against the LORD today, tomorrow the LORD will be angry against the whole community of Israel. If you feel that the land you possess is not sacred, then return to the land that the

LORD has promised us as **an eternal** possession – the place where the LORD's tabernacle is resting – and take possession together with us; but do not rebel against the LORD nor against us by building another altar in addition to the altar of the LORD our God **which is at Shiloh.** Remember when Achan committed an offence by taking things under the divine interdict, did not his wrath fall upon the entire community? That man was not the only one to perish for his iniquity. **All of us will be found guilty for your rebellious act against the Lord."**

The leaders of Reuben, Gad and the half-tribe of Manasseh responded to the heads of the clans of Israel, "God of gods, the LORD God of gods. The LORD – he knows and Israel will know. If it be rebellion, or if it be treachery against the LORD, do not save us today! If we have built an altar to turn away from following the LORD or if to offer on it burnt offerings or meal offerings or peace offerings – let the LORD punish us. But we have done this out of our anxiety because we felt that tomorrow your descendants would say to ours, 'What have you to do with the LORD, the God of Israel? The LORD has made the Jordan a border between us and you, who are the descendants of Reuben and Gad,[1] you have no portion in the LORD. Thus your descendants could make our descendants stop fearing the LORD'.

"It is for this reason we said, 'Let us now act for ourselves by building an altar, **to prevent the possibility of our exclusion from the Lord's portion, and** not for burnt offerings and not for sacrifices but as a testimonial between us and between you and between the generations that come after us that we may participate in the worship of the LORD before him with our burnt offerings and our sacrifices and our peace offerings, so that your descendants will not say in the future to our descendants, "you have no portion

---

[1] They could not say this to the descendants of the half-tribe of Manasseh because, as their brothers who lived in the Promised Land had a portion in the LORD, so too would they be included.

in the LORD." Therefore, we said, 'If they should say to us and to our next generations in the future **such a thing**,' we will say, 'See, the model of the altar of the LORD which our fathers built not for burnt offerings nor for sacrifices but as a testimonial between us and you.' Far be it from us that we should rebel against the LORD and turn away this day from following the LORD to build an altar for burnt offerings, for meal offerings or for sacrifices, as a substitute for the altar of the LORD our God that is before his tabernacle."[1]

Phinehas the priest and the chieftains of the community – the heads of the clans of Israel – who were with him were very pleased to hear these words spoken by the men of Reuben, Gad and Manasseh. Phinehas the son of Eleazar the priest replied to the men of Reuben, Gad and Manasseh: "Today, we know that the LORD is within us because you have not committed any treachery against the LORD. **By what you have said,** you have delivered the people of Israel out of the hand of the LORD **for he has no reason to be angry with us.**" Phinehas the son of Eleazar the priest and the chieftains returned from the tribes of Reuben and Gad from the land of Gilead to the land of Canaan, to the people of Israel, to bring them back word of their mission. What they heard pleased the Israelites. They praised God and thought no more of going up against them to do battle with them or to destroy the land where the Reubenites and the Gadites lived. The Reubenites and the Gadites named the altar: "It is a testimonial between us that the LORD is God."

---

[1] The importance given to centralised worship was probably a later development than is indicated here or in the laws of Moses. It became a prophetic ideal when it became apparent that localised sacrifices led to worship of ancient earth deities which had been prevalent before the Israelite conquest and, sadly, even after it. The exclusive worship of the LORD as the sole and supreme deity was an ideal which was only realised a generation or two before the Babylonian exile in 586 BCE. The Book of Judges gives ample proof of this.

Joshua's farewell address

After many years when the LORD had given security to Israel from all enemies who surrounded her, Joshua was old, well-advanced in years. Joshua summoned the Israelites – their elders, their heads, their judges and their administrators. He said to them, "I am old, well-advanced in years. You have seen all that the LORD your God did to these nations who were before you. It is because the LORD is your God who fights for you. Behold, I have apportioned to you for your possession and inheritance, tribe by tribe, the land of the nations which still remain unvanquished,[1] together with the land of the nations I have wiped out as far as the Great Sea towards the setting of the sun. **Do not fear.** The LORD is your God. He will chase them away from before you and drive them out of your sight. You will possess the land, as the LORD your God has promised you. Therefore, be very resolute in observing all that is written in the scroll of the Laws of Moses and that you stray not from it either to the right or to the left. Do not mix with the nations who yet remain in the country, nor ever mention the names of their gods, nor swear by them, nor serve them nor worship them. You must only hold fast to the LORD your God as you have done until now. Because of this, the LORD has driven out great and powerful nations from before you and not one man has been able to withstand your power until this very day. Each one of you has been able to pursue a thousand enemies but only because the LORD your God is fighting for you as he promised he would.

---

[1] These are listed in Joshua 13:2–6 (see Appendix). One wonders why, with God's power on behalf of the Israelites to wipe out their enemies with hailstones and to extend the time given to Joshua to destroy the Amorites, he could not have conquered the remaining enemy states. The fact must be that the Israelites were unable then to conquer the Philistines, etc. So, while giving credit to God for the other glorious victories, on this failure the narrator remains silent.

"Keep a careful watch over yourselves to love the LORD your God because if you in any way turn your backs on him and attach yourself to those few nations who are still left with you and intermarry with them and fraternise with them, know for sure that the LORD your God will no longer drive out these nations from before you. They will be a snare and trap for you, a scourge to your sides and thorns to prick your eyes – until you perish from off this good land which the LORD your God has given you. You know that today I am going in the manner of the whole earth. **Soon I will die,** but know **even then** with all your heart and soul that the LORD your God has not failed you in fulfilling any of the good things which he promised you. Everything happened for you – not one thing failed.

"But it shall come to pass, just as all the good things that the LORD your God promised you have been fulfilled, so can he bring on you all types of evil until you are wiped off this good land which the LORD your God has given you. **But this will happen only** when you transgress the covenant of the LORD your God which he commanded you; when you go to serve other gods and worship them. Then shall the anger of the LORD blaze out against you and quickly will you be wiped off the good land that he has given you."[1]

Joshua summoned all the tribes of Israel to Shechem; the elders of Israel, their leaders, their judges and their administrators. They presented themselves before God. Joshua said to all of them: "This is what the LORD, the God of Israel says to you,[2] 'Your ancestors in ancient times lived beyond the river [Euphrates], even Terah,

[1] As in Moses' farewell speech, Joshua makes the assumption that the Israelites will act as renegades to God and therefore lose his protection. Fundamentalists will not agree, but it would appear that Joshua's speech is written with hindsight after the destruction of the Israelite kingdoms. It is part of the prophetic theology that Israel's defeats are due not to God's weakness but to their sinfulness.
[2] Here, Joshua speaks as a prophet, enunciating the words of God, as did Moses.

Abraham and Nahor's father, and they served other gods. I took your ancestor Abraham from across the river and led him through all of the land of Canaan. I increased his descendants; I gave him Isaac, Jacob and Esau. To Esau I gave Mount Seir for him and his descendants' possession. Jacob and his children went down to Egypt. Then I sent Moses and Aaron and afflicted the Egyptians after which I brought you out of there. When I brought your fathers out of Egypt and you came to the river, the Egyptians pursued your fathers with chariots and horsemen to the Red Sea. When they cried out to the LORD for help, he caused a darkness to fall between you and the Egyptians and made the sea over-whelm them. You saw what I did in Egypt and you lived in the wilderness for many years. Then I brought you into the land of the Amorites who lived east of Jordan. They fought with you and I gave them into your power and you took possession of their land when I destroyed them in front of you.

'Then did Balak ben Zippor, King of Moab stand up to fight against Israel and he summoned Balaam ben Beor to curse you. I did not want to hear Balaam's curses, so instead he invoked blessings upon you; and I delivered you out of Balak's might. You crossed the Jordan and reached Jericho, and the lords of Jericho, the Amorites, the Perizzites, the Canaanites, the Hittites, the Girgashites, the Hivites and the Jebusites fought against you but I delivered them into your hands. I sent hornets[1] which drove your enemies out before your advance. The two kings of the Amorites were defeated neither with the sword or the bow. So did I give you a land whose soil you had not tilled, and cities which you did not build in which you live, and vineyards and olive groves you did not plant from which you eat.'

Joshua concluded, "Now, therefore, respect the LORD and serve

---

[1] Plagues of hornets were sent to devastate enemy troops even before the Israelites engaged them in battle. The whole tenor of this prophetic speech is to reinforce that Israel's military power was of no relevance to the defeat of the inhabitants of Canaan.

him loyally and with integrity and remove the gods your fathers served east of the Jordan and in Egypt. Serve the LORD! And if it is not to your fancy to serve the LORD, choose this day whom you would serve, be they the gods your fathers served beyond the River or the gods of the Amorites in whose land you now live. As for me and my family, we will serve the LORD!" The people responded, "Perish the thought that we should forsake the LORD for other gods. The LORD is our God – he is the one who brought us and our fathers out of Egypt – the house of bondage – and who performed before our very eyes all those great signs, who sustained us in our entire journey and through all the nations whose lands we crossed. The LORD drove out from before us all the peoples – especially the Amorites who were living in the land. Therefore, we will serve the LORD because he is our God."

Joshua said to the people, "You cannot serve the LORD **together with other gods,** because he is a unique God! He is a passionate God! He will not forgive your transgressions nor your sins. If you forsake the LORD to serve strange gods, he will turn against you and harm you and finish you off, even after he has been so good to you." And the people protested to Joshua, "No, we will only serve the LORD." Joshua confirmed this before the people, "You yourselves are witnesses that you have chosen the LORD to serve him." They replied, "We are witnesses."

- "Now, therefore, put away those foreign gods which you possess and incline your heart to the LORD your God."
- "**Yes,** the LORD our God we will serve, and his voice we will obey!"[1]

So on that day in Shechem Joshua renewed the covenant with the people and placed gave them statutes and ordinances in

---

[1] This is very similar to the affirmation that the Israelites made at Sinai, "All that the LORD has spoken we will do." [Exodus 19:8]

Shechem. Joshua wrote these matters in the scroll of the laws of God. He ordered a great rock to be taken and set up by the tent pole in the LORD's sanctuary. Joshua said to all the people, "See, this rock is a witness against us. It has heard all the words that the LORD has spoken to us. It is therefore a testimonial against you, should you betray your God."[1] Then did Joshua dismiss the people – each person to his inheritance.

After this, Joshua bin Nun, the servant of the LORD, died when he was a hundred and ten years old. They buried him on the border of his allotted land in Timnath-serah, which is in the hill-country of Ephraim, north of the mountain of Gaash. Israel served the LORD all the years of Joshua's reign and all the years of the elders who outlived Joshua and had experienced all the wonders of the LORD which he had performed for Israel.

Now, as to the bones of Joseph which the children of Israel had brought up from Egypt **as he made them promise to do,** they were buried in Shechem which Jacob had purchased from the children of Hamor, the father of Shechem for a hundred pieces of money.[2] This land became the possession of the tribes of Joseph. Also Eleazar the son of Aaron, the **first High Priest,** died and he was buried in the hill belonging to Phinehas, his son, which was allotted to him on Mount Ephraim.

[1] Though Moses in his admonitions to the people of Israel said that he was addressing even those who were not yet born, Joshua is compelled to reinforce the covenant with the generation who has seen God's promises fulfilled. The narrator gives Joshua stature as a prophet, though this aspect is usually ignored.

[2] Genesis 33:19.

The Book of Judges

A Messenger of the Lord came up from Gilgal to Bochim. He said, "I enabled you to go up from Egypt and I brought you to the land which I promised to your ancestors when I said I would never break my covenant with you.[2] But I **also** affirmed that you should make no covenant with the natives of the land **and the gods they serve** but that you should destroy their altars. You did not obey my commandment. How could you have done this! Therefore I also decided, I will not drive the natives out from before you, but they will ensnare you in the worship of their gods which will be like traps for you, **for I will then not honour my covenant with you and you will be defenceless before the people of the land.**"[3] When the Messenger of the Lord said these words to the whole people of Israel, they howled and wept. So the place was called Bochim [Weeping]. There, they offered sacrifices to the Lord.[4]

The people of Israel behaved wickedly in the sight of the Lord for they served the Baalim. They betrayed the Lord the God of their ancestors who had brought them out of Egypt. They turned to strange gods, the gods of the peoples who lived around them, and worshipped them. They made the Lord angry. Indeed they betrayed the Lord to serve Baal and the Ashtaroth [male and

[1] As the first chapter of Judges deals with the territory conquered and unconquered by the Israelites between the death of Joshua and the emergence of the Judges, I have placed it in the Appendix.
[2] God is saying that he would not have broken his contract with the Israelites which was to give them the entire land of Canaan if they had honoured their own commitment to worship him as their only God.
[3] The fact that the Messenger of the Lord speaks in the first person as if he were God can either mean that a phrase such as 'This is the word of the Lord' has been omitted or that the Messenger is a manifestation of God. It would be consistent with biblical theology to believe that God could appear in a corporal form.
[4] See Appendix for Judges 2:6–10 which once again announces Joshua's death.

female fertility gods]. The LORD was incensed against Israel and he delivered them into the hands of raiding marauders and their neighbouring enemies, so they could not defend themselves against their foes. Whenever they engaged in battle, the LORD opposed them just as he had forewarned them. They were in despair.

From time to time, the LORD gave them heroes who delivered them out of the hands of those who raided them **and their homes.** However they did not obey their champion fighters but continued to play the whore with other gods. They worshipped them and quickly strayed from the path in which their ancestors walked in keeping the commandments of the LORD. They did not act faithfully. Still when the LORD sent them champions, the LORD would be with them and would save the people of Israel from the power of their enemies so long as the hero lived. **For, in spite of their betrayal,** the LORD had pity on them because he heard their groaning when they were oppressed and crushed by their enemies. But, as soon as their heroes died, they went astray again and were even more perverted than their ancestors in running after other gods to serve and worship them. They did not exclude any **pagan** practice or corrupt way.[1]

The Lord sends Othniel to save Israel

The people of Israel behaved wickedly in the sight of the LORD. They forgot the LORD their God and served the Baalim and the Asheroth.[2] The LORD was incensed against Israel and he surrendered them to King Cushan–rishathaim of Aram-naharaim. The people of Israel were his subjects for eight years. But when the Israelites cried out for help from the LORD he appointed a saviour

[1] See Appendix for Judges 2:20–3:6 which refers again to the peoples of the land who were not conquered by the Israelites – in order to test Israel's ability to resist the temptation of pagan worship.
[2] A variant of the Ashtaroth – goddesses of fertility.

for them – Othniel ben Kenaz, Caleb's younger kinsman.[1] The LORD's spirit entered into him and he judged Israel. He engaged in battle and the LORD delivered King Cushan-rishathaim of Aram into his power. He triumphed over Cushan-rishathaim. The land was free from foreign domination for forty years. Then did Othniel ben Kenaz die.

Again the people of Israel displeased the LORD by their wickedness. The LORD gave strength to King Eglon of Moab to defeat Israel because they had acted wickedly in the sight of the LORD. He mustered **into his army** the peoples of Ammon and Amalek. He defeated Israel and they took possession of the City of Palm Trees.[2] The people of Israel were subjects to King Eglon of Moab for eighteen years.

When the people of Israel cried out for help to the LORD, he appointed a saviour for them – Ehud ben Gera, a Benjamite who was left-handed **because his right hand was incapacitated**. The people of Israel sent him to bear a tribute of taxes to King Eglon of Moab. But Ehud made for himself a two-edged sword of an arm's length. He tied it to his right thigh but kept it hidden under his tunic. He brought the present closer to King Eglon of Moab. Now he was a very fat man. When he had finished offering the tribute to the king, he sent away those who had accompanied him to convey the tribute. But he then returned **to the king** from Pesilim, near Gilgal and said to him, " Your majesty, I have something secret to tell you." He replied, "Keep it to yourself **for a moment**."

---

[1] For a previous record of Othniel's prowess, see Appendix, Judges 1:12–13.
[2] This is assumed to be Jericho. But Jericho was destroyed according to Joshua. It is a mystery that this contradiction was allowed to remain in Judges once the book was admitted into the Bible.

Ehud delivers a message from the Lord

All his ministers who stood by him were told to leave. Ehud approached him where he was sitting alone in the cool of his upper chamber. Ehud said, "I have a message from God for you." **Shocked by this insolence,** he got up from his seat. Ehud, with his left hand, removed the sword from his right thigh and stuck it into his belly **with such force** that even its handle went in with the blade. **Eglon was so fat** that the flesh closed around the blade. He did not draw the sword out of the belly but let it go through his innards. Ehud **took the key from inside the doors and,** going into the corridor, he closed the doors of the upper chamber after him and locked them. After he left, Eglon's ministers came and saw that the doors to the room were locked. They said, "He must be lowering his tunic in the toilet of the cool chamber. **We had better not disturb him.**" They did nothing and waited in embarrassment for him to open the doors which he did not do. Finally, **concerned for his safety,** they found another key and opened the doors and they found their master lying dead on the floor.

Ehud had taken the opportunity, while they were deciding what to do, to escape. He passed by Pesilim and safely reached the Seirah forest. When he returned home he had horns blown in the hill country of Ephraim **to muster the Israelites to war.** The armies of Israel went down from the hill country with him at their head. He charged them, "Follow me for the LORD has handed over the Moabites, your enemies, into your hands." So they followed him and seized the fords of the Jordan river approaching Moab. They allowed no one to cross them. At that time they killed some ten thousand warriors of Moab – their best and most valiant men. Not one of them escaped **because they were in control of the fords of the Jordan.** So was Moab made subject to the power of Israel. The land enjoyed peace and quiet for eighty years. (After him came Shamgar ben Anath who killed six hundred

Philistines **single-handed** with an ox-goad. He too was a champion for Israel.[1])

When Ehud died, the people of Israel once again behaved wickedly in the sight of the LORD.[2] He handed them over to be subject to King Jabin of Canaan, whose capital was Hazor. The commander-in-chief of his armies was Sisera who lived in Harosheth-goiim. The people of Israel cried for help to the LORD, for Sisera severely oppressed the people of Israel for twenty years. **So great was his army that** he had as many as nine hundred iron chariots. At that time, Deborah [the wife of Lappidoth], a prophetess, was the judge over Israel. She executed judgement at **the place known as** Deborah's palm tree which was between Ramah and Beth-el in the hill country of Ephraim. The people of Israel went up to her for judgement.

"If you go with me, I will go"

She summoned to her Barak ben Abinoam from Kedesh in **the district belonging to** Naphtali and declared to him, "Has not the LORD given this command: 'Go to Mount Tabor and take with you ten thousand men from the tribes of Naphtali and Zebulun **and Issachar.** There at the brook of Kishon I will bring to you Sisera, the commander of Jabin's army. I will deliver him together with his charioteers and infantry into your hands'." Barak replied to her:

– "If you go with me, I will go
    But if you will not go with me, I will not go."

[1] Shamgar is a non-Israelite name. Anath was a foreign goddess of war. He is mentioned in the triumphant war hymn of Deborah [p. 50]. The author of Judges feels compelled to include in his saga of the saviours God sent to help Israel every folk hero, even those who were expropriated from their neighbours. The fact that we are not told of his tribe adds weight to this speculation.
[2] There is no mention here of Shamgar though he was supposed to have judged Israel after Ehud's death.

"I will most certainly go with you
– But, in so doing, your campaign will win you no honour
For people will say that the LORD has surrendered
Sisera into the hand of a woman."[1]

Deborah set off with Barak to Kedesh **where he mustered his troops.** Barak summoned the armies of Zebulun and Naphtali **and Issachar** to Kedesh. Ten thousand went up at his command. Deborah also went with him. (Now Heber the Kenite had severed his relationship with the other Kenites, even from the descendants of Hobab, Moses' father-in-law. He made his settlement as far away as Elon-bezaananim, which is near to Kedesh).[2] Sisera was told that Barak ben Abinoam had gone up **with an army** to Mount Tabor. So he mustered all his chariots – nine hundred iron chariots – and all his forces at Harosheth-goiim to the brook of Kishon. Deborah commanded Barak, "Arise, for this is the day that the LORD will deliver Sisera into your power. **Be not afraid,** for is not the LORD going before you **into battle!**" Barak led his ten thousand men down Mount Tabor **to confront Sisera.**

"Come in my lord, you need not be afraid . . ."

The LORD caused panic to spread among Sisera's charioteers and infantry so that they fell before the swords of Barak's men. Sisera, **in order to escape**, jumped off his chariot to escape on foot. Barak pursued the chariots and the infantry as far as Harosheth-goiim, **Sisera's city.** All of his men were put to the sword – not a man remained alive. Sisera, however, was able to escape on foot to the tent of Jael who was the wife of Heber the Kenite, for there

---

[1] This is prophetic as Sisera is himself killed by a woman, albeit not Deborah.
[2] The reason for this parathentical insertion is clarified later on.

was a treaty of peace between King Jabin of Hazor and the clan of Heber the Kenite. Jael went out to greet Sisera, "Come in, my lord, come into my tent, you need not be afraid."

He went into her tent and she warmed him by covering him with a blanket. He asked of her, "Please, give me some water to drink for I am so thirsty." She opened a skin of milk, gave him it to drink and then covered him again. **Feeling secure becaused of her ministrations,** he said to her, "Stand by the tent opening. If any man should come and ask you, 'Is there any man within?' say that there is not." **When Sisera fell asleep,** Jael, Heber's wife, took a tent peg and hammer in her hands. Softly she moved towards him while he was in a deep sleep. **Before he stirred,** she hammered the peg through his temples, so that it pinned him to the ground. He fainted and died. When Barak was looking for Sisera, Jael ran out to meet him, "Come I will show you the man you are looking for." He went into her tent and there was Sisera – dead with the tent peg through his temples. So did God on that day defeat the forces of King Jabin of Canaan. The Israelites defeated King Jabin in war again and again until he was no longer king over Canaan.

The Song of Deborah

On that day did Deborah and Barak ben Abinoam sing this song,

When chieftains let their hair run wild
    And men rush to take up arms,
I bless Yahweh.
    Hear you kings, give ear O princes.
I am Yahweh's! I will sing!
    I am weaving a song for Yahweh, Israel's god.
Yahweh, when you sauntered out of Seir
    When you marched out of the plains of Edom,
The earth shook, the sky did sink

The clouds could not hold back the rains.
The very mountains quaked before Yahweh
Even Mount Sinai from such a distance
Shook before Yahweh, Israel's god.

In the time of Shamgar ben Anath and Jael
The highways were too dangerous.

Travellers zigzagged through crooked paths.
Israel had no rulers – they disappeared in **fright**
Until I Deborah stood up.
I stood up as a mother in Israel
Before then, they chose new gods
No wonder there were battles by their city gates.

Neither a shield nor spear could be found
Among forty thousand men.

My heart goes out now to the rulers of Israel
Who volunteered **for battle.**

Bless Yahweh
You **who are rich enough** to ride on white donkeys
You who sit on rich rugs,
You who walk leisurely along the way.

Speak of it as loudly
As the sound of the archers
By the watering holes,
Where they speak of Yahweh's valiant deeds
And the virtues of his chieftains
Before Yahweh's people went out to battle.

[Carry on, carry on, Deborah
Carry on, carry on, sing your song.

Stand up, Barak, you son of Abinoam,
Who has taken your enemies into captivity.]

He, **Yahweh**, gave a remnant people domain
Over noble and great nations.

Yahweh gave me dominion over the mighty.
The Ephramites came from amidst the Amalekites.

After you the Benjaminites came **to war.**
From Machir came the chieftains of Manasseh.

From Zebulun came men with scrolls **of**
The names of soldiers registered to do battle.

The chiefs of Issachar rallied around Deborah.
So also did Issachar follow Barak.

From Mount Tabor into the valley they charged
Following the heels of Barak.

Among the clans of Reuben
Were many discussions and debates:

Should they go to war against Sisera?
Why then did you sit among the sheep

Listening to them piping for the sheep
When you should have been with your brothers

Heeding the clarion call to battle?
Yes among the clans of Reuben

There were great searchings of the heart.
Gilead remained on the other side of the Jordan.

Dan why did he stay by the ships?
And Asher by the seashore

Finding rest among the beach coves?
Zebulun – a tribe prepared

To look death in the eye.
So too did Naphtali take the

High ground on the battlefield.
The kings came and did battle.

The Canaanite kings fought
Between Tannach and the waters of Meggido.

They made no profit from the battle.
The stars fought from heaven.

From their courses they fought against Sisera.
The torrents of Kishon swept the enemy away –

The ancient torrent, the raging Kishon.
[March on, my soul, with strength.]

Then did his horse hoofs pound the ground –
Galloping, galloping went his steeds.
Curse **the treacherous town of** Meroz
Says the LORD's messenger.
Let the inhabitants be cursed forever
Because they did not help the LORD –
To help the LORD as his warriors.
Most blessed of women be Jael
The wife of Heber the Kenite –
Most blessed of women who live in tents.
When Sisera asked for water
She fetched him milk.
She served him curds in a princely bowl.
But her hand seized the tent peg.
Her right hand took the workman's hammer.
She struck Sisera with the hammer.
She shattered his head,
Battering the stave through his temples.
By her feet he sank – he fell.
Where he sank – there he lay dead.
Sisera's mother looked through her window
She peered through the lattice:
"Why is his chariot so long in coming?
What delays the clatter of his chariot's wheels?"
The cleverest of her ladies-in-waiting answered her:
[Indeed, she is thinking the same]
"Are they not searching **for loot?**
Are they not dividing the plunder?
A girl maybe two for each soldier,
The spoil of coloured cloths for Sisera –
Indeed embroidered dyed cloths –
Two brocaded scarves to go around the neck
Of every plunderer."
So may all your enemies perish O Yahweh

But let those who love you
Be as the sun rising in its glory.

The land was at peace **and undisturbed** for forty years.

Once again the people of Israel acted wickedly in the sight of
the LORD and the LORD subjected them to the Midianites for seven
years. The Midianites oppressed the Israelites. It was because of
the raids of the Midianites that the Israelites made dens on the
mountains for themselves and dug out caves and made themselves
fortresses. It always happened when Israel was seeding the land
that the Midianites, the Amalekites and marauders from the east
came up to attack them. They laid siege against them, destroyed
the land's produce as far as the approach to Gaza and left no
means for the Israelites to sustain themselves. They were destitute
– without sheep, oxen or donkeys. Their enemies overran them
with their tents and their cattle. They descended like locusts. They
and their camels seemed numberless when they came into the
land to wreak destruction. Israel was utterly crushed by the power
of the Midianites. The people of Israel cried out to the LORD for
help.

When the Israelites began to petition the LORD for help because
of the Midianite hordes, he sent a man – a prophet – to the
Israelites to tell them, "So speaks the LORD God of Israel, 'I raised
you out of Egypt and brought you out of the house of bondage.
I delivered you from Egyptian might, from the subjugation of all
who oppressed you. I drove your enemies out from before you
and gave you their land. I said to you, I am the LORD your God.
You shall not respect the gods of the Amorites in whose land you
dwelt – but you took no notice of what I said. **But, now that you
have forsaken the Amorite gods and have come to me for help,
I will send my Messenger who will appoint a champion to save
you from the Midianites.''**

"Do not worry, you will not die"

The Messenger of the LORD came and sat himself under a terebinth in the fields of Ophrah **near Shechem** which belonged to
Joash the Abiezrite, **a clan of the tribe of Manasseh.** His son
Gideon was beating out wheat in the winepress to deceive the
Midianites **who would not expect that wheat was** being threshed
there. The Messenger of the LORD appeared to him and said, "The
LORD is with you, O mighty warrior." Gideon responded, "**With
all due respect,** my lord, if the LORD is with us, why are we in
such a miserable situation? What has happened to all the miracles
of which our fathers told us? They said, 'Did not the LORD raise
us out of Egypt?' But now the LORD has discarded us and has
subjected us to the oppression of the Midianites." Then the LORD[1]
replied to him, "Go with this courage of yours and save Israel
from the clutches of the Midianites. Have I not sent you!"

– "My Lord, how can I save Israel? My clan is the humblest in
  the tribe of Manasseh, and I am the least in my father's house."
– "Surely, I will be with you. So will you wipe out the Midianites
  as though they were one man."
– "If you could do me this favour, help me to believe with some
  sign that you are really talking to me. Do not go away until I
  return to you with an offering to place before you."
– "I will stay here until you return."

Gideon went into his house and prepared a kid and unleavened
cakes consisting of a bushel of meal. He put the meat in a basket
and the broth in a pot and brought it to him under the terebinth
and gave it to him. The Messenger of God said to him, "Take the
meat and the unleavened cakes and place them on this rock and
pour the broth over it." He did this. The Messenger of the LORD

---

[1] The Messenger of the LORD becomes the LORD himself. To answer Gideon's
rebuff, God is moved to speak directly to him, and not through a mediator.

stretched out the end of his staff which he was holding in his hand to touch the meat and the unleavened cakes. A fire flashed out of the rock and consumed the meat and the unleavened cakes. The Messenger of the LORD disappeared from before his very eyes. Gideon then realised that he was the LORD's Messenger and cried, "Woe unto me, LORD God, I have seen the Messenger of the LORD face to face, **how shall I now live!**"[1] The LORD reassured him, "You will be well. Do not worry. You will not die." Gideon built an altar to the LORD and called it 'The LORD is peace'. It remains to this day in Ophrah which belongs to the Abiezrites.

That same night, the LORD instructed him, "Take a large ox from your father and a seven-year-old bullock. Demolish the altar to Baal belonging to your father. Cut down the Asherah that stands by it and build a proper altar to the LORD your God on top of their fortification. Take the second bullock and offer it as a burnt offering using the Asherah which you have cut down as burning wood." Gideon took ten of his serving hands and did as the LORD had instructed him. **He knew that what he was about to do would be considered a great sacrilege by his family and his neighbours who still worshipped the Baalim and the Asheroth.** Because he was frightened of what his father's kinsmen and the men of his city **might do to him,** he did not feel able to do it by day, so he built it during the night.

"Let Baal defend himself"

First thing in the morning, the townsfolk saw that Baal's altar had been shattered and that the Asherah **tree stump** standing by it had been cut down and that the second bullock had been offered on an alternative altar. They asked each other, "Who has done

[1] The belief was that one could not survive seeing the face of God. This view is expressed in Exodus 33:20, ". . . man shall not see Me and live." The fact that Gideon says this about a Messenger of God suggests that the Messengers were a manifestation of the Godhead.

this?" After some investigation, they learnt, "Gideon ben Yoash has done this." The townsfolk then said to Joash, "Deliver your son to us so that he may be executed because he has demolished Baal's altar and has cut down the Asherah which stood by it." Joash protested to all those who confronted him, "Are you fighting the cause of Baal, will you **seek to** save him **as god?** He that takes his side will be dead before the morning light. If he is a god let him contend with the person who destroyed his altar." For this reason, from that day onward, Gideon was also called Jerubbaal [Baal Will Contend] because it was said, "Let Baal contend with the one who broke down his altar."

Once again the Midianites and the Amalekites and the hordes from the East joined together. They passed over the plains and set up camp in the valley of Jezreel. But now the spirit of the LORD enveloped Gideon like a garment and he blew the horn **to rally the Israelites** to battle. His clan of Abiezer gathered together to follow his lead. He sent emissaries throughout the territory of the tribe of Manasseh and they too heeded his call. He also sent emissaries throughout the territories of Asher, Zebulun and Naphtali and they were already coming up to meet the Manassites.

Gideon addressed the supreme God, "If you intend to save Israel through my might as you have promised, see: I am now putting a fleece of wool on the threshing floor. If **in the morning** there be dew only on the fleece but dry on the ground surrounding it, I will know that you will deliver Israel through me, just as you said you would." So it happened. The next morning when he arose at early light and pressed the fleece together, he wrung out of the fleece a bowl full of water. Then Gideon said to the supreme God, "Do not be angry with me if I speak again to put **to you** another test **to see whether you will support me.** This time, let only the fleece be dry but the ground full of dew." God did so that night: **the next morning** it was only dry on the fleece but dew was on the ground.

Then Jerubbaal, that is Gideon, and all his forces assembled at dawn and set up camp by En-harod. The Midianite camp was north of them by Gibeath-moreh in the valley of Jezreel. The LORD instructed Gideon, "You have too many men with you for me to deliver the Midianites into your power. **For, were I to do so when your forces are so great,** the Israelites will boast of their power rather than of mine. They will say, 'Our own strength, **not the Lord's,** has delivered us.' So proclaim within earshot of all your army, 'Whoever is afraid and trembling **at the prospect of battle,** let him turn back from the battleground'." **With that offer,** twenty-two thousand men left. Ten thousand remained steadfast.

The LORD again told Gideon, "There are still too many men. Take them down to the river bank and I will set an elimination test for you there. I will tell you who are to follow you and who are not to go with you." So he took the men to the river bank. The LORD then said to Gideon, "All who lap up the water with their tongues as do dogs, place on one side. Do the same to those who bend down on their knees to drink." The number of those that lapped the water by putting their hands to their mouths was three hundred. All the rest of the men knelt on their knees to drink the water. The LORD said to Gideon, "By the three hundred men that lapped the water will I save you by delivering the Midianites into your grasp. Let all the others return to their homes." So most of the men collected their provisions along with their battle horns. Gideon sent all these Israelites to their homes, only retaining the three hundred men.[1] The Midianites were encamped in the valley below them.

That very same night, the LORD said to Gideon: "Up, descend on the Midianite camp for I am delivering it into your grasp. But,

[1] Throughout the biblical narratives, the theme of God delivering the many into the hands of the few is a recurrent one. It is to prove the prophetic faith that the LORD alone is the source of Israel's salvation. It is the very reverse of Bismarck's statement that God is on the side of the army with the most battalions.

if you are still anxious, go down secretly with Purah your servant to hear what the Midianites are saying. Then your morale will be bolstered to attack the camp." Gideon went down with Purah to the last outpost of the armed men of the camp. The number of Midianites, Amalekites and the hordes from the East was so great that they appeared in the valley like swarms of locusts. Also, they had camels beyond counting like sand on the seashore. **Gideon and Purah disguised themselves as Midianites and covered their faces with shawls against the night breeze.** When Gideon drew near **to a camp fire,** he heard a soldier relating a dream to his companion, "I had this dream in which a flat and circular loaf of barley bread was flipping over from side to side in the Midianite camp. It came to a tent, as if to attack it and made it collapse by turning it upside down." His comrade said, **"As the Israelites are farmers, the loaf of barley bread** must **be a symbol of** the sword of Gideon ben Joash, the Israelite. **Your dream is an omen that** by his might God will defeat Midian and the entire army."

When Gideon heard the dream and its interpretation, he worshipped **God for the reassurance that the dream of the Midianite had given him;** he returned to the Israelite camp and shouted, "Come, the LORD has handed into your hands the armies of Midian." He divided his men into three companies. He gave each of them horns and a pitcher in which to conceal their torches. He commanded them, "Keep your eyes on me and do whatever I do. When I reach the outposts of the camp, do as I do. When I and all those with me blow our horns, then blow your own horns all around the camp. **As you do,** cry out **as loudly as you can:** 'For the LORD and for Gideon'."

The defeat of Midian without a blow being struck

Gideon and the hundred men with him reached the outpost of the camp at the beginning of the middle watch, when the new sentries had been posted. **Following Gideon's lead,** they blew their horns and broke the pitchers which they held. When the three companies blew their horns and broke their pitchers and held torches in their left hands while their right hand held the horns which they were blowing, they cried out, "A sword for the LORD and for Gideon!" Every one of them remained steadfast at his place around the camp. **Though they did not engage in battle, the soldiers in the Midianite camp were so terrified by the blowing of horns and the breaking of the pitchers which sounded like the beating of camel hoofs against the ground,** they all ran out of their tents, screaming as they fled.

Gideon's men kept blowing the three hundred horns. **Because of the confusion and panic,** the LORD turned every man's sword against his fellow throughout the camp. All their forces fled as far as Beth-shittah and on to Zererah as far as the outskirts of Abelmeholah near Tabbath. Now the men of Israel from the tribes of Naphtali, Asher and Menasseh joined together to pursue the Midianites. Gideon sent messengers throughout the hill country of Ephraim with this request: "Join us in the attack against the Midianites and take control of the water crossings all along the Jordan down to Beth-barah. The men of Ephraim rallied together and took control of the water crossings along the Jordan as far as Beth-barah. They pursued the Midianites and captured two commanders of the Midianites who were named Oreb [Raven) and Zeeb [Wolf]. Oreb was executed at the place which became known as the Rock of the Raven and Zeeb was executed at the place which became known as the Winepress of the Wolf. They brought the heads of Oreb and Zeeb to Gideon on the other side of the Jordan, **where he was in pursuit of Zebah and Zalmunna, the kings of Midian.**

The men of Ephraim were upset with Gideon for not calling on them sooner to do battle with the Midianites. They demanded of him, "Why have you treated us in this way? Why did you not send for us when you went to fight with Midian?" They rebuked him with great ferocity. Gideon had not rallied them earlier because he was afraid that they would have taken control of the campaign. They would not have listened to the instructions of the Lord and would have led him to defeat. Now, when victory was his, they could easily complain that they had not been involved from the outset. But Gideon won them over by saying, "What is my success in this war compared to yours? Is not the gleaning of Ephraim better than the vintage of my own clan Abiezer?[1] See, God has given into your hands the commanders of the Midianites, Oreb and Zeeb. What have been my military successes compared to yours?" Their anger towards him subsided when they heard these words of compliment.

Gideon with his three hundred men reached the Jordan and crossed over it. They were faint with hunger yet maintained their pursuit. On the way he said to the men of the town of Sukkoth, "Please, let me have some bread for the troops who are with me. They are faint with hunger and we are chasing Zebah and Zalmunna, the kings of Midian." The leaders of Sukkoth refused, "Are Zebah and Zalmunna already in your power that we should give food to your forces? What if you fail, will they not return through our town and destroy us for helping you?" Gideon replied, "If that is the case, when the LORD has handed over to me Zebah and Zalmunna, I will do as they would have done. I will throw you naked on a bed of thorns and briars and trample you underfoot." From there he went up to Penuel, and also asked them for food. The men of Penuel responded just as had the men of

---

[1] The metaphor is that the small grapes left over after the collecting of the vineyards for wine of the land of Ephraim were tastier than the best grapes of Gideon's land.

Sukkoth. So he warned the men of Penuel, "When I return victorious, I will tear down this tower."

Zebah and Zalmunna were in Karkor. The fighting men with them numbered some fifteen thousand – all that was left of the hordes of marauders from the East. One hundred and twenty thousand of their fighters had already been slain. Gideon approached them by the nomadic route east of Nobah and Jogbehah and attacked their army, for they thought that they were safe there. Zebah and Zalmunnah ran away but he pursued them. He captured the two kings of Midian and routed their enemies. Gideon ben Joash returned from the battle by the Heights of Heres.

He captured a young man from the townsfolk of Sukkoth. He interrogated him and had written down the names of all the leaders and elders of Sukkoth – numbering some seventy-seven men. When he came to the men of Sukkoth, he mocked them, "Here are Zebah and Zalmunna regarding whom you taunted me with the words, 'Are Zebah and Zalmunna already in your power that we should give bread to your men who are faint?'" He seized the elders of the town, **had them stripped** and wild thorns and briars **were thrown over them and they were trampled underfoot.** So did he teach the townsfolk of Sukkoth a lesson. So too did he, **as he had warned,** overthrow the tower of Penuel and slay its **fighting men.** He then asked Zebah and Zalmunna, "Who were the men you slew in Tabor?" They replied, "They looked just like you as made out of one mould – aristocratic as the sons of a king." Gideon lamented, "They were my brothers, my mother's sons. As the LORD lives, had you allowed them to live, I would not have killed you." He ordered Jether, his first-born, "Stand up and kill them." But the lad did not draw his sword because, being only a youth, he was nervous. Zebah and Zalmunna pleaded with him, "You should strike us down for strength goes along with manliness. **Why should we suffer a prolonged death because we are slain by an inexperienced hand?**" So Gideon stood up and killed Zebah and Zalmunna and took the royal crescents that hung on their camels' necks as **trophies of war.**

The Israelites hailed Gideon, "Rule over us. You, your son and your son's sons, for it was you who brought us salvation from the Midianites." But Gideon rebuffed them, "I will not rule over you, nor will my son. The LORD **alone** will rule over you. Do you not understand? **It was the Lord who defeated the Midianites, how else could I have destroyed tens of thousands with only three hundred men had not the** LORD delivered them into my hands!" Gideon said to them, "I would **however** make a request of you, that each of you give me the earrings which you have taken as booty." For the enemy, being nomads, wore golden ear-rings. They replied, "Willingly we give them to you." They spread out a garment. On it every man threw the ear-rings from his plunder. The weight of the golden ear-rings for which he asked was a thousand and seven hundred golden shekels.[1] **This was given to him** in addition to the crescents and the pendants and the purple worn by the kings of Midian as well as the jewelled collars worn by their camels. **From his booty,** Gideon had an ephod made which he placed in his town of Ophrah. **As it was the breastplate to be worn by the High Priest, it was considered holy.** Because of this, the Israelites would **eventually** worship it. So did it become a snare to Gideon and his family.[2] In this way the Midianites were vanquished by the people of Israel. Never again did they hold their heads up high. The land enjoyed peace for forty years during the time of Gideon.

Jerubbaal – Gideon ben Joash – retired to his own home **from where he ruled Israel.** Gideon sired seventy sons because he had many wives. A concubine of his living in Shechem bore him a son whom he called Abimelech. Gideon ben Joash died at a ripe

---

[1] A shekel weighed half an ounce. According to the current value of gold, this would have been worth about £150,000.

[2] This may have been the justification for the fall of Gideon's household.

old age. He was buried in the sepulchre of Joash his father, in Ophrah of the Abiezrites. As soon as Gideon was dead, the people of Israel were seduced by the Baalim and made Baal-berith their god. The people of Israel forgot the LORD their God who had saved them from all their enemies round about them. Neither did they show any gratitude to the family of Jerubbaal-Gideon for all the good he had done for Israel.

The massacre of the sons of Gideon

Abimelech ben Jerubbaal-Gideon went to Shechem to his mother's kinsmen. He spoke to them and to the kinsmen of his mother's father, "Please speak to all of the citizens of Shechem: What is better for you, that all the seventy sons of Jerubbaal rule over you or that only one man rule over you? Also remember that I am your bone and flesh." So did his mother's kinsmen speak to the citizens of Shechem. They were persuaded to follow Abimelech for they thought, "He is our kinsman." They gave him seventy pieces of silver from the Shrine of Baal-berith, with which Abimelech hired base and empty-headed louts. He took them with him to his father's house in Ophrah and executed his brothers, the sons of Jerubbaal, on one large rock, all seventy of them excepting Jothan, the youngest son of Jerubbaal who had managed to hide himself.

All the citizens of Shechem joined together with those of Beth-millo to make Abimelech king by the terebinth by the column of pillars in Shechem. When this was told to Jothan, he proceeded to stand on the top of Mount Gerizim. He raised his voice and shouted: "Listen to me you citizens of Shechem that God may listen to you. Once the trees wanted to anoint a king over themselves. They said to the olive tree, 'Be our king.' The olive tree said, 'Seeing that I am honoured by God and man for yielding rich oil, should I give this up to rule over the trees?' Then the trees went to the fig tree, 'Be our king.' The fig tree said, 'Should

I give up yielding my sweet fruits in abundance to rule over the trees?' Then the trees went to the vine and said to her, 'Be our king.' The vine said to them, 'Should I give up my wine which gives good cheer to God and man to rule over the trees?' Then all the trees went to the bramble bush, 'Come, be our king.' The bramble bush said to the trees, 'If you really want to anoint me king over you, you must come and take protection under my shadow. If not, let my bramble become a fire and burn up the cedars of Lebanon. **For Abimelech is like a bramble bush. Can he give protection to trees greater than himself? Like the bramble bush, his only power is the danger that, in the great heat of the day, a flame will kindle his thorns and set a flame to a forest of trees greater than it'.**

"Do you think you have acted faithfully and with integrity in making Abimelech king? Have you dealt fairly with Jerubbaal and his family according to what he deserved? My father fought for you and risked his life for you and delivered you from the oppression of the Midianites. Today you attacked my father's family. You have killed his seventy sons on one large rock and have made Abimelech, the son of Jerubbaal's handmaid, king over Shechem because he is your kinsman. If you think he acted faithfully and with integrity with Jerubbaal and his descendants, then rejoice in Abimelech and let him rejoice in you, **his subjects.** But if you have not acted well, let fire come out of Abimelech and consume the citizens of Shechem and Beth-milloh. And let Abimelech be consumed in that same fire." Jothan then fled to Beer where he stayed because he was in fear of Abimelech, his brother.

Abimelech was ruler over Israel for three years. God stirred up bad feelings between Abimelech and the citizens of Shechem, so they betrayed him – **in order that retribution should occur** for the violence done to the seventy sons of Jerubbaal and that their blood might be on **the head** of Abimelech, their brother, who killed them, and also on **the heads of** the citizens of Shechem, who gave him the means to kill his brothers. The citizens of Shechem organised highwaymen on the top of hills to rob all those who came along their roads to see **and bring tribute to** him. Abimelech was told what was happening.

Gaal ben Ebed and his kinsmen came and settled in Shechem, whose citizens trusted **him to be their ally in their rebellion against Abimelech. Without anxiety of incurring Abimelech's anger,** they went into the fields and harvested their vineyards. They trod the grapes, made a feast and entered the shrine of their god. They ate and drank and cursed Abimelech. Gaal ben Ebed declared, "Who is Abimelech and who is Shechem **that it should be under his sway** that we should serve him? Is he not the son of Jerubbaal? And of what consequence is Zebul, his commander? You should be serving the men of Hamor, the founders of Shechem! Indeed, why should we serve Abimelech! If only the people accepted my rule, I would remove Abimelech." He sent this message for Abimelech **through Zebul,** "Muster up your largest army and come out to fight me."

When Zebul, the governor of the city, heard these words of Gaal ben Ebed, he became furious. He sent messengers to Abimelech in Arumah to inform him, "Gaal ben Ebed and his kinsmen have come to Shechem and are inciting the people against you. My advice is for you to proceed witth your men at night and encamp in the fields **near Shechem.** As soon as the sun rises, advance against the city. When he and his men come out to attack you, you will do to him as it pleases you." Abimelech and his men set out at **night** and lay in wait against Shechem in four companies. **The next morning** Gaal ben Ebed looked out from the entrance of the city gate. Then Abimelech and the men with him got up and began to march. When Gaal saw the men, he said to Zebul: "See, men are coming down from the hill tops." Zebul reassured him, "What you see is the shadows **of the trees on** the hills which look like men." But Gaal insisted, "Look, there are people marching down the centre of the fields and another group is marching by the road of Elon-meonenim." Then Zebul chided him, "Well now, what of your boasting, 'Who is Abimelech that we should serve him?' Are they not the people of whom you were so contemptuous? So go out now and fight with them."

Jothan's curse is fulfilled

Gaal led the citizens of Shechem to do battle with Abimelech. **They were defeated** and Abimelech pursued after them when they fled. Many fell wounded even close to the city gate. Abimelech's headquarters were in Arumah. **So by this strategy was** Zebul able to drive out Gaal and his kinsmen and they no longer lived in Shechem. One morning, when the people of Shechem were leaving the city **to do their normal business**, Abimelech took his men and divided them into three companies and lay in ambush in the fields. When the Shechemites were leaving the city, he attacked and struck them down. Abimelech and the company with him quickly advanced and stood by the entrance of the city gate to cut off and strike down those who were seeking to escape the attack of the other two companies. So Abimelech attacked the city throughout the day. He captured it and killed the people in it. He razed the city and sowed it with salt.

When the citizens of the Tower of Shechem, **which is Beth-millo, heard about the massacre of Shechem,** they hid themselves in the underground room of the Shrine of El-berith. When Abimelech was told that all the leading citizens of the Tower of Shechem had huddled together, Abimelech and his men went onto Mount Zalman. Abimelech took an axe in his hand and chopped down a tree branch and placed it on his shoulder. He ordered the men who were with him, "What you have just seen me do, quickly do the same." All his men chopped down branches and following Abimelech put them against the underground room **of the Shrine** and set fire to them. So did all the citizens of the Tower of Shechem – Beth-millo – die, also, some one thousand men and women. **So** was the curse of Jotham against the citizens of Shechem and Beth-millo fulfilled.

After his success and lusting for more blood, Abimelech advanced against Thebez. He laid siege against it and captured it. Within the town was a strong fortress to which all the men, women and children fled. They shut themselves in it and proceeded to the roof of the fortress. Abimelech advanced against the fortress to attack it. He approached the fortress door to set it aflame. But one woman threw down a large millstone on to Abimelech's head which broke his skull. He shouted to the youth who carried his armour and ordered him, "Draw your sword and kill me that men should not say of me, 'A woman slew him'." His young man thrust his sword through him and he died. When the Israelites saw that Abimelech was dead, they all **left Thebez and** returned home. So did God achieve retribution for the wickedness of Abimelech for killing his seventy brothers. Also for the wickedness of the men of Shechem did God achieve retribution on all of them. Thus was the curse of Jotham ben Jerubbaal fulfilled.

After Abimelech's death, Tola ben Puah ben Dodo, a man from the tribe of Issachar, protected Israel. He lived in Shamir in the hill country belonging to the tribe of Ephraim. He **ruled and judged** Israel for twenty-three years. When he died he was buried in Shamir. After him, Jair the Gileadite **ruled and** judged Israel for twenty-two years. He had thirty sons who used to ride on thirty ass-colts. They possessed thirty towns which are called 'Haroth-jair' [the villages of Jair] to this very day which are in the territory of Gilead. When Jair died, he was buried in Kamon.

After this the Israelites did that which was wicked in the sight of the LORD. They served the Baalim and the Ashtaroth, the gods of Aram, the gods of Zidon, the gods of the Moabites and Ammonites, and the gods of the Philistines. They rejected the LORD and did not serve him. The LORD's anger was inflamed against Israel, so he had them subjected to the might of the

Philistines and to the might of the Ammonites. They oppressed and crushed the Israelites from that year **of Jair's death.** For eighteen years were the Israelites oppressed, especially those Israelites who were in Transjordan in the land of the Amorites which is in Gilead.

The Ammonites crossed the Jordan to fight against the tribes of Judah and Benjamin and against the clans of Ephraim. The Israelites were deeply demoralised. The Israelites cried out to the LORD, "We have sinned against you because we have rejected our God and have worshipped the Baalim." The LORD said to the people of Israel[1], "Did I not deliver you from the Egyptians, the Amorites, the Ammonites and the Philistines? When the Zidonians and the Amalekites and the Maonites oppressed you and cried out to me, I delivered you from them. In spite of this, you have rejected me to serve other gods. **I have had enough!** I will save you no more. Go and petition the gods you have chosen, let them save you in your times of trouble!" The Israelites said to the LORD, "We know that we have sinned. Do whatever pleases you, but please deliver us this day." They disposed of their alien gods and began to serve the LORD, and the LORD's life was saddened by Israel's misery.

[The Ammonites mustered their armies and encamped in Gilead. The Israelites joined together and encamped at Mizpah. The men, the officers of Gilead, asked one another, "What man will lead us into battle against the Ammonites? That man will be made the ruler of all the people of Gilead."] Jepthah the Gileadite was a powerful and courageous man. He was the son of a prostitute. Gilead was Jepthah's father. Gilead's wife bore him two sons. When his wife's sons grew up, they evicted Jepthah with these words, "You will have no inheritance from our father's estate, for you are a son of another woman." Jepthah left his kinsmen

---

[1] It is interesting that there is no record of an intermediary here – no messenger or prophet.

and lived in the land of Tob. **Slowly but surely because of his might,** men with no employment joined Jepthah and went out with him **to raid the countryside.**

The Ammonites had decided to make war against Israel. When they were attacking the Israelites, the elders of Gilead went to bring Jepthah out of Tob **to lead them into battle for they had heard of his prowess.** They said to him, "Come, be our chief to lead us in the battle against the Ammonites."

– "Did you not despise me? Did you not allow my brothers to turn me out of my father's house? So why do you come now when you are in trouble?'
– "That is just why we have come to you. Join us. Fight the Ammonites and we will make you the head of all those who live in Gilead."
– "If you bring me back home to fight the Ammonites and the LORD delivers them into my power, will you make me your head?"
– "The LORD is witness between us. According to whatever you say, we will do."

Jepthah went with the elders of Gilead and the people made him their head chieftain. Jepthah confirmed his agreement **with the elders of Gilead** before the LORD in Mizpah.

Jepthah's vow

Jepthah sent emissaries to the king of the Ammonites with these words, "What complaint do you have against me, that you have come to wage war in my territory?" The king of the Ammonites sent these words back with Jepthah's emissaries, "It is because the Israelites took away my land when they came out of Egypt from the Arnon as far as to Jabbok and all along the Jordan. Now restore these towns peaceably **and I shall withdraw my army**." Jepthah sent back his emissaries carrying this reply, "So says

Jepthah: Israel did not steal the land of Moab nor the land of Ammon. When Israel came out of Egypt they journeyed through the wilderness up to the Red Sea until they reached Kadesh. At that time Israel sent emissaries to the king of Edom with this request, 'Grant us permission to travel through your territory.' But the king of Edom did not agree. He made the same request of the king of Moab. He too refused. So Israel remained in Kadesh. Then he had to journey through the wilderness and go around the territories of Edom and Moab, **going south along the western border of Edom and then through the wilderness northwards,** east of Edom where he pitched his tent on the other side of the Arnon river, but they never came into Moab territory.

"Israel sent emissaries to King Sihon of the Amorites who reigned in Heshbon. Israel's message was: 'Please, allow me to pass through your territory to my place **of settlement,** but Sihon did not permit Israel to pass through its land. Rather did Sihon muster his men, pitch his war camp in Jahaz and attack Israel. The LORD, the God of Israel, delivered Sihon and all his troops into the hands of Israel, who destroyed them. So did Israel capture the land of the Amorites who lived in the country at that time. They took possession of the entire territory from its southern border on the Arnon river to its border on the Jabbok river, encompassing the wilderness up to the Jordan river. So did the LORD, the God of Israel, dispossess the Amorites in favour of his people Israel. And now you would claim it as yours. You claim the lands which Chemosh,[1] your God, has granted you. But those territories the LORD our God has captured for us we will keep!

"**Now you propose to war against us to recover the lands of**

---

[1] The god of Moab. The Amorites had conquered Moab. The Ammonites who had united with Moab (remember that according to Genesis 19:30–38, Moab and Ammon were brothers who were conceived by Lot's two daughters after their incestuous relationship with him). Now the king of the Ammonites was claiming back the land which Moses had conquered from the Amorites who had previously conquered their fellow tribe of Moab.

Moab. What makes you think that you are mightier than Balak ben Zippor who was king of Moab **when Moses, the Lord's servant, was leading us to the land that the Lord our God had vowed to give to our ancestors.** He never dared to fight the Israelites. Israel dwelt in **the territories of the Amorites which the Lord our God delivered to Moses, his servant** – Heshbon and its villages, Aroer and its villages and all the towns along the Arnon river for three hundred years. Why did you not seek to recover them during all that time? **You know that** I have done you no wrong but you do me wrong to engage me in battle. Today, the LORD will be the one to judge between the people of Israel and the people of Ammon."

The king of the Ammonites disregarded the message that Jepthah sent to him. The spirit of the LORD inspired Jepthah. He went through Gilead and the territory of Manasseh, passing from Mizpeh which is in Gilead **after mustering his troops** into the territory of Ammon. Jepthah made a vow to the LORD: "If you will deliver the armies of Ammon into my hand, I swear that, whatever is the first to come out of the doors of my home to greet me if and when I successfully return from battle with the Ammonites, it will belong **to the Lord. I will sacrifice it as a burnt offering.**"[1] Jepthah advanced into the territory of the Ammonites to confront them in battle. The LORD delivered them into his hand. He struck them down from Aroer even unto Minnith, all of twenty towns, as far as Abel-cheramim. They were severely beaten. So were the Ammonites humbled before the Israelites.

When Jepthah returned home to Mizpah, Oh was it not his daughter who was the first to come to greet him dancing with

[1] This was an incredibly rash vow. What did he think it could be? His dog perhaps, or a slave. He knew that there was a likelihood that the victim would be human. The prophets attacked the act of human sacrifices. This must be a very ancient tale which precedes the more elevated morality in the Mosaic codes which even forbids the tearing of one's flesh as an expression of bereavement.

timbrels in her hands. She was his one and only, he had no other son or daughter. When he saw her, he tore his clothes in grief,

> "Woe, woe, you have weakened my limbs
> **You have taken my strength away**
> **I cannot stand,** I am bent low.
> You have become the source of my affliction
> With my mouth I tempted the LORD.
> **I have made a vow**
> **To sacrifice the first one to greet me**
> And there is no going back."

She replied to him,

> "My father, you have spoken to the LORD
> You must do to me according to your vow.
> For the LORD has taken vengeance on your behalf
> Against your enemies – the Ammonites."

She continued to speak,

> "Only allow me this one favour.
> Leave me be for two months.
> Let me go down from the public places
> And into the hills
> To weep over my wasted virginity –
> I and my friends with me."

He said, "Go!" and sent her away for two months. She and her companions went away and wept for her wasted virginity in the hidden places of the mountains. At the end of two months she returned to her father who did to her in accordance with the vow he had made.[1] She had never lain with a man. It became a custom among the Israelite maidens for them to mourn over the daughter

---

[1] The narrator is unable to write boldly that Jepthah sacrificed his daughter.

of Jepthah the Gileadite **by singing elegies of praise** for four days every year.

Not long after this event, the men of the tribe of Ephraim[1] assembled and went northwards to speak to Jepthah, "Why is it that you did not call upon us to join you in battle against the Ammonites? **We are so angry,** we would burn your house down in flames." Jepthah retorted, "I and my people were sorely distressed by the Ammonites. We had previously asked for assistance, but you did not come to deliver us from their might. When I realised that you would not save me from them, I took my life in my hands and I went to encounter the Ammonites and the LORD submitted them to my might. So why do you come up to me today to attack me?"

Jepthah mustered all the men of Gilead and fought against the Ephraimites. But the Gileadites defeated the Ephraimites because they taunted them, "You are the most cowardly among the tribes of Ephraim and Manasseh, **the first to run from battle.**"[2] To prevent their escape, the Gileadites took control of the crossings of the Jordan river. When a runaway soldier said, "Allow me to cross over," the Gileadites said to him, "Are you an Ephraimite?" If he said "No", they would say to him, "Say now 'Shibboleth'."[3] When he said 'Sibboleth', because he could not pronounce it correctly, they seized him and killed him by the crossing of the Jordan. As the result of that battle forty-two thousand Ephraimites were slain.

Jepthah ruled over Israel for six years. When Jepthah the Gileadite died he was buried in one of the towns in Gilead. After him, Izban from Bethlehem ruled over Israel. He sired thirty sons and thirty daughters. He sent off his thirty daughters to marry

[1] Ephraim was the more powerful brother tribe of Manasseh – descendants of Joseph – who were furious that they were deprived of the glory and plunder in the Ammonite defeat.

[2] The taunt makes no sense in the original Hebrew. My interpretation is based on the *Targum*, the Aramaic translation.

[3] The most common meaning is 'an ear of corn'.

men of other tribes and brought from other tribes thirty women to marry his sons. **So did his influence spread throughout the tribes of Israel.** He ruled Israel for seven years. At his death, he was buried in Bethlehem. Elon the Zebulunite, after him, ruled Israel for ten years. When Elon died, he was buried in Aijalon in the territory of Zebulun.

After him, did Abdon ben Hillel, the Pirathonite from Ephraim, rule over Israel. He sired forty sons and from them had thirty grandsons who would ride on seventy large donkeys.[1] He ruled over Israel for eight years. Abdon ben Hillel the Pirathonite died. He was buried in Pirathon in the territory of Ephraim in the hill country also inhabited by the Amalekites.

Samson the mighty Nazirite

Again the people of Israel behaved wickedly before the LORD who submitted them to the rule of the Philistines for forty years. There was a man of the town of Zorah from a clan of the tribe of Dan, whose name was Manoah. His wife, being barren, did not bear him any children. A Messenger from the LORD appeared to the woman. He said to her, "I know you are barren and have not borne a child, but you are to conceive and give birth to a son. Now be diligent **to what I say.** You are not to drink wine or liquor nor eat any food forbidden **to the Nazirite.** When you become pregnant and give birth to a son, no razor must touch his head for the lad will be a Nazirite unto God even from the womb **until his death.**[2] He will begin the task of saving Israel from the might of the Philistines."

The woman hastened to tell her husband, "A man of God came

---

[1] These rounded figures of the children of Izban and Abdon suggest that these are legendary heroes of whom there was little information available to the narrator.

[2] Individuals would take on the vows of the Nazirite discipline for a period [Numbers 6:1–21]. St Paul did so. See *People's Bible: Luke & the Apostles* p. 127 Samson was to be a Nazirite throughout his life.

to me. His appearance was that of a Messenger from God. He was
so awesome that I did not ask him where he came from nor did
he tell me his name. But he said to me, "You will conceive and
give birth to a son. Now, do not drink wine or liquor and eat no
forbidden foods. For the lad will be a Nazirite unto God from the
womb to the day of his death." Manoah prayed to the LORD,
"Please, my lord, let the man of God whom you sent come to us
again and instruct us on how to raise the lad who is to be born."
God answered Manoah's prayer and the Messenger of God
returned to the woman. She was sitting in the field but Manoah,
her husband, was not with her. The woman ran as quick as she
could to tell her husband, "Look, the man that came to me the
other day has come again." Manoah stood up and followed his
wife and came to the man and asked him, "Are you the same
man who previously spoke to my wife?"

– "I am."
– "When your promise is fulfilled, how shall we behave towards
  him?"
– "Whatever I said to the woman, let her obey. She must not
  eat anything which comes from the grape-vine, nor should she
  drink wine or liquor nor eat any forbidden food. She must
  follow everything I commanded her. **The life of the lad is in
  the hand of God.**"
– "Allow us to detain you so that we may prepare a kid for you
  to eat."
– "Even if I allow you to keep me for a while, I will not eat your
  food. If you intend to make a sacrifice, you should offer it to
  the LORD."

Because Manoah did not realise that he was a Messenger from
the LORD[1], Manoah asked the Messenger of the LORD, "What is

---

[1] This fortifies my conviction that 'angels' looked like men and had no wings or
haloes. They were awe-inspiring but could have been charismatic prophets.

your name, so that when your words come to be fulfilled we can honour you **with a reward?**" The Messenger of the LORD rebuffed him, "Why do you ask my name, seeing that it is a hidden mystery?" **Hearing this,** Manoah took a kid together with a meal offering and sacrificed it on a rock to the LORD who performed a miracle as Manoah and his wife looked on **in amazement.** When a flame burst out from the sacrificial altar towards heaven, the Messenger from the LORD ascended into the flame which was coming from the altar. When Manoah and his wife saw this they threw themselves with their faces onto the ground. The Messenger of the LORD never again appeared to Manoah and his wife.

Manoah knew that this was a Messenger of the LORD. Manoah moaned to his wife, "We must certainly die for we have seen God!"[1] But his wife reassured him, "If the LORD wished to kill us, would he have accepted our burnt offering or meal offering, or would he have shown us all this, or would he now have told us such things?" So did the woman give birth to a son whom she called Samson.[2] The lad grew and the LORD blessed him. The spirit of the LORD began to inspire him when he was living in Mahaneh–dan which is between Zorah and Eshtaol.

When he had grown into manhood, Samson went down to Timnah where he saw a woman of the daughters of the Philistines. He returned to his father and mother and told them, "I have seen a woman who is of the daughters of the Philistines. Now, obtain her to be my wife." His father and mother protested, "Is there no woman among the daughters of your kinsmen or among all my people that you go to fetch a wife from the uncircumcised Philistines?" But Samson replied to his father, "**Never mind,** obtain her for me, because she is the right one for me." His father and mother took comfort that this must be the will of

[1] This suggests that the Messenger of God is a physical manifestation of the Godhead who had the power to take on any form.
[2] In Hebrew *Shimshon* derived from *Shemesh* meaning Sun.

the LORD to find an excuse to harm the Philistines, for, **as you know,** the Philistines were the overlords of the Israelites.

Samson, his father and mother were going down to Timnah. When they reached the vineyards of Timnah, a young lion began to roar against Samson. The spirit of the LORD gave him great strength. **He seized it** and tore it apart as if it had only been a kid – and **this he did** without any weapons. **But his parents had fled from the vineyards** and he did not tell his father and mother of his feat of strength. So Samson then went to speak with the woman and he was mightily pleased with her. **He left her while his father began negotiations over the marriage contract.** When he returned to take her **to be his wife,** he went to see what had become of the lion's carcass. A swarm of bees had made a hive in its body and it was full of honey. He scraped it out with his hands and happily ate it as he was walking along. When he came to his father and mother he gave what was left to them, but did not tell them that he had scraped it out of the lion's body. His father went down to the woman **to obtain her agreement to the marriage.**

When she agreed, Samson made a feast, for such was the custom of the young men in Philistia. When they saw the stature of the man, the Philistines sent thirty men to accompany him **and to keep him out of trouble.** Samson challenged them:

"Let me give you a riddle.

If you can answer it within seven days of the feast

With the correct answer

I will give you thirty linen tunics

As well as thirty changes of festive clothing.

But if you cannot solve it

You will give me thirty linen tunics

And thirty changes of festive clothing."

They replied, "Tell us your riddle so that we may hear it."

"Out of the carnivore came food

And out of the fierce one came sweetness."

After three days they were not able to solve the riddle. During the week they threatened Samson's wife, "Persuade your husband to tell you the solution to the riddle. If not, we will burn you and your father's house with fire. Did you invite us here to bankrupt us?" So Samson's wife wept in front of him crying, "You hate me, you do not love me. You have posed a riddle to my countrymen. Why won't you tell me the answer?" He defended himself, "See, I have not told it to my father or my mother. Shall I tell it to you?" She wept for the remainder of the seven days while the feasting lasted. **Worn out by her weeping,** he told her on the seventh day because she kept putting more pressure on him. She immediately told the riddle's answer to her countrymen.

On the seventh day the townsfolk said to him before the setting of the sun:

"What is sweeter than honey

What is fiercer than a lion?"

He replied:

"If you had not ploughed with my heifer

You would not have solved my riddle."

The spirit of the LORD filled him with great strength. He went down to Ashkelon, **one of the five great Philistine cities,** and killed there thirty men. He plundered their homes and gave thirty changes of clothing to those who had answered the riddle. His anger **against his wife** was so great that he returned to his father's home. Samson's wife was then given to one of his **thirty** companions who had acted as his best man. **But Samson did not know this.**

Some time later, in the time of the wheat harvest, Samson went to be reconciled with his wife. He brought her a kid as a present. He said, "I will go to my wife into our bedroom." But her father would not permit him to go in, "I thought that you hated and despised her. For this reason I gave her to one of your groomsmen. **But do not be angry.** Her younger sister is more beautiful than she. Please take her in her place." Samson said to them, **for the**

other members of the family had joined her father, "Now will I be finished with the Philistines for the mischief I will do to them!" Samson left them. He captured three hundred foxes and tied each one of them to the next by its tail and put a torch between the knots tying the two tails. After setting the torches on fire, he chased them into the fields of standing grain belonging to the Philistines.[1] They burnt up both the sheaves and the standing grain as well as the vines and olive trees.

The Philistines asked, "Who is responsible for this?" They answered, "It was Samson, the son-in-law of the Timnite, because he took his wife and handed her over to one of his groomsmen." So the Philistines came up to Timnah and burnt her and her father's house with fire.[2] Samson said to the Philistines, "If this is the way you intend to behave, I will be avenged. Only then will I cease."[3] Single-handedly he went through the Philistines striking them down one by one by the hip or by the thigh. Then he went down to secure himself **against capture from the Philistines** in the rock cave of Etam **in the territory of Judah.**

The Philistines went up and pitched their camp in the territory of Judah by Lehi. The men of Judah demanded, "Why have you come up against us?" They replied, "To arrest Samson. **We have come to** requite him for what he has done to us." Three thousand men of Judah went to the rock cave in Etam and said to Samson, "Do you not know that we are subjects of the Philistines? What are you doing to us?"

– "As they did to me, so have I done to them."

---

[1] This gargantuous feat of tying foxes by the tails with torches held in the knots to be allowed to run loose is also found in other ancient literature.

[2] The Masoretic Hebrew text has the Philistines burning her father as well as her. A most extraordinary act of vengeance.

[3] What is Samson criticising? Their barbaric behaviour or the fact that they have avenged themselves against the source of Samson's anger rather than against Samson; or did Samson still consider the woman they burnt as his wife!

– "We have come to tie you up and to hand you over to the Philistines."
– "Swear that you will not kill me yourselves."
– "No, we will not, but will tie you up securely and deliver you into their hands, but we will not kill you."

They bound him with two new ropes and brought him up from the rock cave. When he was brought to Lehi, the Philistines shouted when they saw him captive. The spirit of the LORD filled him with great strength and the ropes that were tying his arms became as soft as flax that had been burnt by fire and the ropes fell from off his hands. He saw a jawbone of an ass. He took it into his hand and killed a thousand men with it. Samson cried out:

"With the jawbone of an ass –
Arse piled on arse
With the jawbone of an ass
I have slain a thousand men."[1]

After this shout of victory he threw the jawbone away. That place was called Ramath-lehi [Jawbone Heights]. He was exceedingly thirsty. He petitioned the LORD, "As you have won this great victory through my might, will you now let me die of thirst and thus still be captured by the uncircumcised **Philistines**?" So God made a divide in the basin at Lehi and water began to flow out. When he had drunk enough, his spirit revived and his strength returned. For this reason the water basin was named En-hakkore [The Spring of the Crier] which is in Lehi until this very day. For twenty years, Samson was Israel's hero during the days when the Philistines were dominant in the land. **He caused havoc when they went to attack the Israelites but they could never capture him.**

---

[1] In the Hebrew, Ass is *Hamor* and piles is also *Hamor*. He killed the Philistines with such speed that they fell on top of each other. I have tried to capture the flavour of the wordplay.

Samson carries away the gates of Gaza

Once Samson went to Gaza where he met a whore and went into her room. The Gazites heard, "Samson has come here." They prevented his escape by closing all the gates and lay quietly in wait for him by the gates the whole night **because they did not know where he was.** They said, "When morning comes **and he comes out** we will kill him." Samson, however, only stayed there until midnight. He got up at midnight, took hold of the gates of the city along with their two posts and plucked them up with the bar **which locked them together.** He heaved them onto his shoulders and carried them up to the top of the mountain before Hebron **a distance of some forty miles.**

After this he loved a woman who lived in the valley of Sorek whose name was Delilah. The lords of all the Philistine city states went to see her and said, "Use your seductive power to find out the source of his colossal strength, and how we can restrain him so that we can tie him up in order to torture him. **If you succeed in this,** each one of us will give you eleven hundred pieces of silver."

Delilah **chose her moment and** asked Samson, "Tell me please, what is the source of your great strength so you may be bound and weakened?" **Samson laughed, thinking once again the Philistines would use a woman to trick him. "I will play with them."** Samson said to her, "If they were to tie me with seven new bowstrings which were never dried then I would become as weak as ordinary men." The lords of the Philistines sent her seven new bowstrings which had never been dried and she tied him up with them. She had men lying in wait in the next room. She awoke him with these words, "Samson, the Philistines are attacking you." He broke the bowstrings as a tow rope when it is burnt by fire. So the source of his strength was not known.

Delilah pouted at Samson, "You make fun of me and tell me lies. Please tell me now how you might be bound up." **He thought,** does she think me stupid that I should tell her the source of my strength so that she might tell the Philistines? I shall tease her some more. He told her, "If they tie me up with new ropes which have never been used then will I be as weak as ordinary men." So Delilah took new ropes which had never been used and bound him with them. She then shouted at him, "The Philistines are attacking you, Samson." Once again there were men lying in wait in the next room, **but before they approached**, he broke them off from his arms as though they were threads.

Delilah tried again, "Until now, you have made fun of me, telling me nothing but lies. Tell me how you might be tied up **so that you cannot wrench yourself free." He continued to play with her and lied again.** "If you weave seven locks of the hair of my head with the web." So, **while he slept,** she did so and fastened the locks she wove with a pin **so that it could not become loose.** She cried out: "Samson, the Philistines are attacking you." Waking up from his sleep, he plucked away the pin of the beam and the web **which held his hair together.** She wept, "How can you say that you love me when your heart is not united with mine – **when you do not trust me?** You have made fun of me three times and have kept from me the secret of your strength." So she pestered him day after day **pleading with him to trust her if he loved her.** She kept urging him until he **was at his wit's end** and sick to death.

One night as he lay in bed with her, he went to embrace her and to enter her. She said, "No, I will not lie with you. You do not love me and I will not give you my love unless you trust me and tell me the source of your great strength." So, he emptied out his heart to her, "No razor has ever touched my head, for I have been a Nazirite dedicated to God even in my mother's womb. If I am shaven, **I will have broken my vow to God, his spirit will forsake me** and I shall become as weak as ordinary men."

As Delilah knew that he had poured out his whole heart to her, she sent to call for the lords of the Philistines with these words, "You can now come up for he has poured out his whole heart to me." The lords of the Philistines went to her bringing the money **they promised her** with them. She **gave him a special potion which** made him fall asleep on her knees. She **quietly** called a man and ordered him to shave off the seven locks of his hair from his head. She then began to strike him. All his strength disappeared. Then she said, "Samson, the Philistines are attacking you." He woke up from his sleep thinking, "I will go out as before and give myself a good shake **and my strength will return,"** because he did not know that the LORD had left him. The Philistines seized him and plucked out his eyes. They took him to Gaza and they chained him with brass fetters and made him grind corn in the prison house. But his hair began to grow again after it had been shaven.

"Let me die with the Philistines"

All the lords of the Philistines came together to offer a great sacrifice to Dagon, their god and to celebrate for they said, 'Our god has delivered Samson our enemy into our hands." When the people saw Samson **grinding corn in the prison house**, they praised their god and declared, "Our god has delivered our enemy into our hands, he who was destroying our country by killing so many of us." When **in the midst of feasting**, they became very merry, they cried out, "Bring us Samson so that we may tease him." They brought Samson out of the prison house and they made fun of him, **turning and twirling him around and causing him to stumble because he was blind.** Then they stood him between two pillars. Samson asked the lad who was holding him by his hand, "Allow me to touch the pillars which hold up this hall so that I can lean on them."

Now, the hall was packed with men and women. Also, all the lords of the Philistines were there. There were even some three thousand men and women standing on the roof looking at

Samson while they were making fun of him. Samson then cried out to the LORD, "LORD God, please remember me, please give me strength only this once, O God that I may be avenged of the Philistines for removing my two eyes." Samson grasped the two centre pillars on which the hall rested. He leaned on them, his right hand on one and his left on the other. Samson prayed, "Let me die with the Philistines." He used all his strength to push the pillars further apart. **The pillars began to move and gave no support to the roof,** so that the great hall collapsed on the lords and all who were in it, so that those who died by Samson's death were more numerous than those he had killed during his lifetime. His kinsmen and all of his father's house went to Gaza. They took his body[1] and brought him up and buried him between Zorah and Eshtaol in the burial place of Manoah his father. He had protected Israel for twenty years.

Now, after Samson's death, there were no heroes to fight for Israel. The tribes did not unite against their enemies. There was lawlessness in the land. The people made graven images of God whom they worshipped. They did not go to the priests appointed by the LORD but made their own priests do their bidding. They desecrated the name of the LORD and did what was evil in his sight. They had no respect for man or for God. There was **such** a man from the hill country of Ephraim whose name was Micayehu.[2] He confessed to his mother, **"You know the bag with** eleven hundred pieces of silver[3] that was stolen from you, which made you in my hearing curse the thief? **I confess** the silver is with me, I stole it. **I will return it to you. Please remove your**

---

[1] Amongst all the other mourning Philistines looking for the bodies of their relatives, they would not have been noticed.

[2] Meaning: he who is like Yahweh. Usually translated in its abbreviated form as Micah. In regard to the man's character, his name is a misnomer. Out of regard for the great prophet Micah, I employ the longer form for this scoundrel.

[3] This is the same amount that each of the Philistine lords promised Delilah. This and the proximity of the story to that of Samson's leads one to identify Micayehu's mother with Delilah.

curse from me." His mother rejoiced, "Blessed be my son of the LORD." He gave back the eleven hundred pieces to his mother, who said, "I will certainly dedicate the silver for the LORD's purpose by giving it to my son to make a sculptured cast in which to pour the molten silver so you will **in that form** have the silver back." So, when he handed the silver to his mother, she took two hundred pieces of silver and gave them to a silversmith who from a sculptured cast made a molten image of silver. It was set in Micayehu's house.

Now this man Micayehu had turned one of his houses into a shrine to God. He made an ephod, a **metal and jewelled breastplate to be worn by the priest from which he could learn the will of the Lord** and household idols **to bring prosperity.** He even consecrated one of his sons to be a priest. **He did this to enrich himself from all those who wanted to make petitions and presentations to the Lord. He could do this because** in those days there was no king reigning over Israel. Every man **behaved lawlessly** doing whatever he felt right in his own interest. A young man came from Bethlehem in Judah who, while he lived amongst the Judeans, was a Levite. He had left his town – Bethlehem of Judah – to find a place where he could settle down **with a secure income.** He reached the hill country of Ephraim and stopped in the course of his journey at Micayehu's house. Micayehu asked him, "From which place do you come?"

– "I am a Levite of Bethlehem in Judah and I go to look for **work and** a place in which to settle."
– "Stay with me and be my **spiritual** father and priest. I will pay you ten pieces of silver a year as well as a change of clothing and all your food."

The Levite agreed. He was happy to live with the man and the young man was for him as one of his sons. Micayehu consecrated the Levite who became his priest and remained in his house.

Micayehu was pleased with himself. "Now I know that the LORD will favour me because I have a Levite as my priest."

The slaughter of the citizens of Laish

As I said, in those days there was no king in Israel **to unite the tribes and to judge them and lead them into battle. Every tribe had to fend for itself.** In those days the tribe of Dan[1] still had no permanently assigned settlement in which to live because in those days no land had been allotted to them as was the case with the other tribes of Israel. So the men of Dan sent from their clan five men from their total number – extremely valiant men from the villages of Zorah and Eshtaol – to spy out the land and to explore it **so that they might find a permanent settlement**. Their instructions were, "Go, explore the land." They reached the hill-country of Ephraim, even to the house of Micayehu and took up lodgings there. When they were in the house, they recognised the dialect of the young man who was the Levite. **He was from Judah so why was he now in Ephraim?** They turned to speak to him, "Who brought you here, what are you doing here and what benefits do you have here?"

– "This is how Micayehu has treated me. He hired me and I have become his priest."
– "**In that case,** please consult God so that we might know whether we will succeed in our mission."
– "Go in peace, for the LORD will tell you where to go."

The five men left and arrived at Laish and looked over the people who lived there. They saw that they lived in ease and prosperity as did their neighbours, the Sidonians, living tranquil and trusting lives for there was no one in their vicinity who wielded authority over them capable of humiliating them in any

[1] The reader should remember that Samson was also a Danite.

86

manner. They lived some distance from the Sidonians. They were self- sufficient and had no associations with any other peoples. They returned to their kinsmen in Zorah and Eshtaol **who asked them what they saw.** After they told them, they were asked, "What say you **that we should do?**" They replied, "Up, let us attack them. We have seen their land. It is very rich. Do not dally nor be indecisive about going to take possession of it. When you arrive there you will find the people complacent **and unsuspecting. They will not be able to resist us.** And the land is of a wide expanse. God has given it into your power – a place which lacks nothing of everything to be found on earth."

Six hundred men from the clan of the Danites set out from Zorah and Eshtaol, fully armed and ready for battle. They went and encamped first in Kiriath-jearim, in Judah. For this reason that place is named Mahaneh-dan (Dan's Encampment) until this very day. It is still behind Kiriath-jearim. From there they passed into the hill-country of Ephraim where they came to the house of Micayehu. The five men who went to spy out the land of Laish said to their kinsmen, "Did you know that in these houses you will find an ephod, household idols, and engraved molten image. Consider how you would like to deal with this news!"

They stopped there, turned into the house of the young Levite – the dwelling also of Micayehu. They asked him how he was. The six hundred men armed with their weapons of the tribe of Dan stood watch by the gate's entrance. When the five spies went into the shrine and took the graven image, the breastplate, the household idols and the molten image, the priest was standing by the gate with the six hundred fully armed men. When the men had gone into Micayehu's house and brought out the engraved metal breastplate, the household idols and the molten image, he asked them, "What are you doing?" They replied, "Hold your peace, put your hand over your mouth **and be silent.** Come with us and be for us a **spiritual** father and priest. Is it better for you to be priest in the house of one man or to be priest for an entire tribe of the family of Israel?'' The priest accepted their proposal with enthusiasm. He took the breastplate, the household idols and the molten image and walked in the centre of the people. When they proceeded to leave, they put their little ones, their cattle and **wagons carrying** their possessions in front of them.

When they were a good distance away from the house of Micayehu, the men of his house and his neighbours' households, joined forces and overtook the Danites and began shouting at them, **"Hey there, hey there!"** The Danites turned to face them and rebuked Micayehu, "Why have you come with so many men?"

- "You take away my god which I had made and the priest, and just walk off **with them.** What is left for me? **How am I to make a living?** Then you ask of me, 'What is your problem?' "
- "Do not let us hear the sound of your voice anymore. We have some excitable fellows who could become angry and attack you. Your life and the lives of your family could then join those of your dead ancestors, **so you may think it best to return home quietly."**

The Danites then carried on. Micayehu saw that they were too strong for him so he **and his neighbours** turned back towards home.

So, without interference, they were able to steal the idols that Micayehu had made and his priest and reached Laish, to a people who were peaceful and innocent. They rampaged through the city burning houses and putting to the sword every person. They then burnt down the city. No one came to their assistance because the nearest city was Sidon which was far away and they had no dealings with anybody **but themselves.** Laish was in the valley near Beth-rehob. The Danites rebuilt the city and lived in it. They called the city Dan, after the name of their ancestor Dan who was Israel's (Jacob) son. But the city was originally called Laish. The people of Dan raised up the molten image for themselves **as**

a representation of God, and, **the young man who was Micayehu's priest,** Jonathan, the son of Gershom, the son of Moses, he and his descendants were priests to the tribe of the Danites until the exile of Israel **by King Sennacherib.** But Micayehu's graven image which he had made remained in their shrine all the time that God's house was established in Shiloh.[1]

The rape of the Levite's concubine

It transpired in those days, when there was no king reigning over Israel, there was a Levite living on the furthest side of the hill-country of Ephraim who took a woman from Bethlehem in the territory of Judah to be his concubine. His concubine went a-whoring against him and left him to return to her father's home in Bethlehem. She remained there for four months. Her husband went after her to persuade her gently to come back. He was accompanied by his servant and a few donkeys. She invited him into the house of her father who was delighted to meet him. His father-in-law, the girl's father, kept him there for three days. They ate and drank and lodged together.

On the fourth day, they woke up early in the morning to leave, when the girl's father said to his son-in-law, "First refresh yourself

---

[1] The tale of Micayehu, the young Levite and the Danites in search of territory to conquer is a gruesome but fascinating tale. A crooked son, perhaps of Delilah who betrays Samson for a pot of silver, sets up an idolatrous shrine focussing on the worship of an image molten in silver. He employs a nomadic Levite – remarkably Moses' grandson – to keep the shrine. The regalia of the shrine as well as the priest are stolen by the warring Danites who are about to descend on the peaceful folk of Laish to destroy them in order to conquer their land for their own settlement. Divine disapproval of their behaviour is indicated by the refrain: "In those days when there was no king reigning over Israel every man **behaved lawlessly** doing whatever he felt was right in his own judgement." The shocking brutality of the Danites leaps off the pages to stun the reader. This illustration of greed and ruthlessness and the tale which now follows indicates the justification for a central authority to impose law and order on the tribes of Israel.

with some food and afterwards go on your way." So they both sat down and ate and drank together. The father of the girl then said, "Come, agree to stay the night and enjoy yourself **with a feast of good food and wine.**" The man got up to go, but his father-in-law persuaded him to stay, so he lodged there a further night. He got up early on the fifth day to leave and again the girl's father pleaded, "First refresh yourself and stay until evening." So both of them ate. When the man got up to leave with his concubine and his servant, the girl's father implored him, "Look, the day is becoming dark and night approaches, lodge here tonight and enjoy yourself. Tomorrow you will get up early, go on your way to your own home."

The man refused to stay another night but got up and left. They were approaching Jebus – that is Jerusalem. He had with him his saddled donkeys and also his concubine. When they were close to Jebus, and night had begun to fall, the servant said to his master, "Please let us stop in the city of the Jebusites and lodge there." But his master refused, "We will not turn into a foreign city that does not belong to the Israelites. We will travel to Gibeah, **an Israelite town.** Come, let us go to a place there. We will lodge either in Gibeah or Ramah." So they travelled on and made their way. The sun set on them when they were close to Gibeah which belonged to the tribe of Benjamin. They stopped there to find lodgings in Gibeah. Finally, he had to go and rest in the town square because no one agreed to let them lodge in their home.

Now an old man who was also from the hill-country of Ephraim was returning from his work in the fields. He was dwelling in Gibeah even though, **unlike himself**, the men of the town were Benjamites. He looked up and saw the travellers in the town square. The old man asked, "Where are you heading and where do you come from?"

– "We were travelling from Bethlehem in Judah to the furthest end of the hill-country of Ephraim from where I come. You see, I had gone to Bethlehem, but I am now going to the LORD's sanctuary **in Shiloh**, but there is no one prepared to take me into his home. **It is not as if** I did not have with me straw and grain for our donkeys and food and wine for myself, this woman and the lad who is with me. We lack nothing, **but shelter for the night.**"

– "Fare you well, let me be responsible for all your needs. You will not sleep in the town square."

He brought him to his home, gave fodder to the donkeys. They washed their feet and ate and drank. As they were enjoying themselves, certain crude fellows from the town surrounded the house and pounded at the door. They demanded of the old man who was the master of the house, "Bring out the man who has come to your house that we may lie with him." The man, the master of the house, went out to them and pleaded with them, "No, my brothers, please do not act so wickedly as this man has entered my house **to enjoy my hospitality and I am responsible for him.** Do not commit such an abominable act. **Anything else would** be better than this: Here is my daughter who is still a virgin and his concubine. I will bring them out to you. Abuse them and do what you wish with them but do not act so abominably with this man."[1]

The men would not listen to him. So the Levite, **who was frightened for his life,** grabbed his concubine and pushed her out to them. They lay with her and abused her the whole night until dawn when they let her go. At first light the woman came and fell down at the door of the man's house where her master was and lay there till it became very light. Her master got up in the morning, opened up the doors of the house to go on his way,

---

[1] The old man's speech reveals several aspects of the crude morality of the times: the high regard given to hospitality, the aversion to homosexuality and the low status of women. This tale is very reminiscent of the desire of the Sodomites to rape Lot's divine guests. See *People's Bible, Genesis* p. 39.

without any regard for his concubine whom he had given up as lost. **When he opened** the doors, the woman who was his concubine had collapsed at the door, her hands lying across the threshold. **Without a sense of shame or concern**, he said to her, "Get up and let us be going." But she could not answer **for she was dead.** He placed her on his donkey and proceeded to return to his home. When he arrived, he took a knife, took hold of his concubine and cut her up, limb by limb, into twelve pieces and dispatched them throughout the territories of Israel, **explaining what had happened to her.**

When they saw it, they exclaimed **to each other**, "Such barbarism as this has not occurred nor has been seen since the day the people of Israel left the land of Egypt until this very day. Consider what has happened, deliberate and give us your view." **The elders of Israel took counsel and made their decision:** the people of Israel prepared for war. They assembled, united in purpose, as one man, from Dan to Beersheba including the land of Gilead to **do** the LORD**'s work** at Mizpah. The chieftains of all the people and every tribe of Israel joined the assembly of God's people – four hundred thousand infantrymen who were swordsmen. The Benjaminites heard that the Israelites had assembled at Mizpah.

The leaders of the tribes of Israel said to the Levite, "Tell us how this wickedness came about." The Levite, the husband of the murdered woman, answered, "I came to Gibeah that belongs to Benjamin, I and my concubine, to lodge. The men of Gibeah came to attack me. They surrounded the house intending to kill me. They raped my concubine and she died.[1] Then I took my concubine, cut her into pieces and dispatched the parts of her body throughout the country to wherever the Israelites lived, for the Benjaminites had acted abominably and with depravity in Israel. Here you are – all Israelites: deliberate and decide what is to be done."

---

[1] The Levite does not give the full story for this would have revealed his cowardice in sacrificing his concubine for his own safety.

All the people were of one mind: "Not one of us will go back to his tent nor return to his home **until we have achieved our purpose.** This is how we will act against Gibeah. By lot we will determine who will attack it. Now, ten of every hundred, a hundred of every thousand and a thousand of every ten thousand will forage for the others when they go to attack Gibeah in Benjamin to punish them appropriately for the abomination they have committed in Israel." So were all the men united with a common purpose.

The tribes of Israel sent messengers throughout the land of Benjamin with these words: "What wickedness is this that has occurred among you? Now, hand over those brutish men who are in Gibeah so that we may execute them and erase this evil from Israel." But the Benjaminites did not agree to accede to the demand of their kinsmen – the people of Israel. The men of Benjamin assembled together from all their towns to Gibeah to do battle with the Israelites. The Benjaminites who left the towns for war were twenty-six thousand swordsmen besides those who lived in Gibeah who numbered six hundred choice warriors. Of all these men, seven hundred were left-handed and could sling stones at a single hair and not miss.

The number of the men of Israel, besides Benjamin, were four hundred thousand swordsmen – all of them warriors. The Israelites got up and proceeded to Beth-el to enquire of the LORD: "Who of us should be the first to do battle against the Benjaminites?" The LORD answered: "First Judah." The Israelites rallied in the morning and encamped by Gibeah. The Israelites arrayed themselves in battle order against Benjamin. The Benjaminites sallied forth from Gibeah and **with their** sling shots and swords hewed down to the ground twenty-two thousand Israelites.

The people of Israel did not lose heart and once again arrayed themselves for battle as on the previous day. But their elders went up to Beth-el and wept before the LORD until the evening. They enquired of the LORD, "Shall we again proceed to attack the people of Benjamin, our kinsmen?" The LORD said: "Attack them!" The Israelites advanced against the Benjaminites on the second day. The Benjaminites sallied out of Gibeah and again hewed to the ground eighteen thousand Israelites – all of them swordsmen. Then all the Israelites – the whole people – went up and came to Beth-el and wept and sat **in mourning** before the LORD. They fasted until the evening. They sacrificed burnt offerings and peace offerings before the LORD. The Israelites enquired of the LORD – for the ark of the covenant of God rested there in those days and Phinehas ben Eleazar ben Aaron ministered to it – with this petition, "Shall we again advance to do battle against the people of Benjamin, our kinsmen, or shall we retreat?" The LORD said. "Attack, for tomorrow will I deliver them into your power."

The Israelites set ambushes around Gibeah. On the third day the Israelites advanced to attack the Benjaminites and arrayed themselves for battle against Gibeah as on the previous days. The Benjaminites went out against them and were drawn away from the town. They began to strike and kill the men as they had done previously, in the field and on the highway some thirty Israelites on the way to Beth-el and Gibeah. The Benjaminites shouted, "They are being beaten by us just as before!" But the Israelites said, "Let us flee in order to draw them away from the town towards the highways."

The main body of the Israelite army left their positions and put themselves in battle array at Baal-tamar near Gibeah. The Israelites in the ambush around Gibeah stormed out of Maarehgeba, **a wooded area behind the town.** Ten thousand of the best Israelite warriors reached Gibeah. The battle was becoming bloody and the Benjaminites did not realise how close they were to defeat. The LORD struck down the Benjaminites before Israel. The Israelites destroyed on that day twenty-five thousand Benjaminites – all swordsmen. The Benjaminites then saw that they were beaten. But the Israelites retreated before the Benjaminites because they relied upon the ambush they had set up against Gibeah. The men of the ambush quickly invaded the town of Gibeah and put to sword all the townsfolk. A signal had been agreed between the Israelite warriors in the field and those who were lying in ambush – to add to the confusion by causing a great column of smoke to arise out of the town.

When the Israelites began to retreat from the battle, the Benjaminites began to strike and kill the Israelites – some thirty fighters. Then they thought, **"The tide of the battle has turned.** They are falling down before us as in the first forays." But when the column of smoke began to rise out of the town, and the Israelites stopped retreating **and resumed taking the offensive,** the Benjaminites were startled and they saw that catastrophe was looming over them. They turned their backs to the Israelites and fled towards the wilderness, but they could not escape the Israelites. The Israelites who now had left the city also began to attack the Benjaminites together with other Israelite contingents. They surrounded the Benjaminites and pursued them. They overtook them at Menuhah far away from Gibeah, where the sun is seen to rise **were you looking at it from Gibeah.** Eighteen thousand Benjaminites were killed – all valiant fighters. Those who survived retreated and fled into the wilderness seeking to reach the Rock of Rimmon. On the highway, the Israelites cut down five thousand men as the gleanings **of wheat strewn on the field.** They chased them as far as Gidom and killed two thousand of them. On that day twenty-five thousand valiant swordsmen of Benjamin were slain. Six hundred men who had retreated, fleeing into the wilderness, reached the Rock of Rimmon and stayed in its protective enclosure for four months. The Israelites turned back from pursuing them to attack the Benjaminites who had remained in their towns. They put to the sword everything they saw, even the cattle. They burnt down every single town they found. **So not one person, man, woman or child, was spared.**

The conspiracy to save the tribe of Benjamin

Now, in the day of the great destruction of the tribe of Benjamin, the Israelites had sworn, "Not one of us shall give our daughter to be a Benjaminite's wife." **Four months passed** and the elders of the Israelites came to Beth-el and sat there **in mourning** until the evening crying and weeping copiously **for they regretted wiping out the entire tribe of Benjamin, except for the six hundred swordsmen who were at the fortress of Rimmon.** They cried out, "O LORD, God of Israel, why did we bring this to pass that today one tribe should be missing in Israel?" The next day the elders of the people got up early, built an altar and sacrificed burnt offerings and peace offerings **and they took counsel with each other what to do about the future of Benjamin.**

The elders of the Israelites asked, "Who was there among all the tribes of Israel that came not to our assembly when we approached the LORD **and vowed to attack the Benjaminites for the abomination they had committed in Israel?" They asked this question** because they had made **on that day** a solemn oath concerning those who had not come up to the assembly of the LORD at Mizpah, "They shall surely be put to death." **The Israelite elders were struggling for a solution to revive the tribe of Benjamin,** for the Israelites repented over what they had done to Benjamin, their kinsmen, "Woe, there is one tribe cut off from Israel today. And how shall we provide wives for the Benjaminites who remain as we have sworn not to give them our daughters to be their wives?"

But they said to each other, "Who among the tribes of Israel that did not come up to the LORD at Mizpah **and who did not make this vow and whom we swore to punish with death?"** They realised that none of the men living in Jabesh-gilead had joined the camp of those who had assembled there, for when the men were being numbered, none of those who lived in Jabesh-gilead were there. So, the council **of elders** despatched twelve thousand of their best men with these orders: "Go and strike with your swords the inhabitants of Jabesh-gilead even the women and infants. These are your exact orders: you will wipe out every male and every woman who has lain with a man." **After fulfilling their mission, after slaying every man, woman and child, they kept alive** four hundred young virgins whom they found among the inhabitants of Jabesh-gilead, who had not had sexual intercourse with any man. They brought them **weeping and desolate** to the camp at Shiloh, **which is north of Beth-el,** which is in the land of Canaan.

The elders of the whole council sent a delegation to the Benjaminites that were in the fortress of Rimmon to offer them peace. So the **six hundred** Benjaminites returned at that time and were given the women whom they had kept alive from Jabesh-gilead. But as there were only four hundred women, there were not enough for them. The people regretted what they had done to Benjamin, because now the LORD had created a gap among the tribes of Israel. Then the elders of the council deliberated, "How do we provide wives for those – **the two hundred** – that remain **without women,** in view of the fact that all the women of Benjamin were slaughtered? **We must help them.** They that have escaped destruction must inherit that which belonged to the tribe of Benjamin for no tribe must be blotted out of Israel. Still we cannot give them our daughters for we have sworn, 'Cursed be he who gives his daughter as wife to Benjamin.' Consider: there is an annual feast to the LORD in Shiloh north of Beth-el, on the east side of the highway that goes towards Shechem from Beth-el, on the south of Lebonah."

Accordingly, they gave these instructions to the Benjaminites, "Go and lie in ambush in the outlying vineyards. When you see **the girls of Shiloh come out to join in the dancing, leave the vineyards and kidnap for each one of you a wife from the girls** of Shiloh and take them back to the territory of Benjamin. Now, when their fathers or brothers come to remonstrate against us **for instructing you to do this,** we will plead with them **on your behalf** by saying to them, 'Be generous to them for our sake because in battle **at Jabesh-gilead** we did not take enough women to give to each man a wife, neither could **we nor** you give our daughters to them for then you would have been guilty **of breaking our oath and be cursed. Now that they have kidnapped them, neither you nor we are guilty and the tribe of Benjamin is saved'."**

The Benjaminites were reassured that they would not be slaughtered as were their kinsmen when they did not surrender those who raped the Levite's concubine to the Israelites. So did the Benjaminites do. They took for themselves wives according to the number they required from the dancing women. They carried them off and took them to their territories and built towns for themselves and lived in them. **Having concluded this matter to their satisfaction,** the Israelites then left Shiloh with every man returning to his tribal seat, to his family and to his home. **You must remember that such things could only happen because** in those days there was no king reigning over Israel. Every man **behaved lawlessly** doing whatever he felt was right in his own judgement.[1]

---

[1] This tale is even more gruesome than the previous one: A Levite goes to retrieve his whoring concubine. He persuades her to return only to sacrifice her to fellow-Israelites from the tribe of Benjamin in order not to be buggered. He does not go out to look for her. She crawls back to the door of his lodgings after continuous abuse throughout the night. On opening the door to return home, he sees her lying with her arms stretched over the threshold. With no compassion, he says, "Let's go," but of course she is dead. Feeling robbed of his property, he carves her up in twelve pieces and demands action from his fellow-Israelites. He lies to them, reveals only half-truths omitting his own cowardliness, perhaps unnecessarily because they might have acted as he had. The elders feel that the Benjaminites' behaviour cannot go unpunished. Their refusal to surrender the culprits leads to the genocidal attack against all the Benjaminites, provoked by their slaughter of over forty thousand of their own warriors. Suddenly – the irony of the narrator ought not to be missed – they regret having wiped out an entire tribe, with the exception of the six hundred men who escaped. They cannot regenerate the tribe because they have also

sworn not to give any Benjamites their daughters for wives. With the same sense of rough justice they despatch Israelite warriors to commit genocide against the inhabitants of Jabesh-gilead for not mustering their men to attack Benjamin. Only four hundred virgins are kept alive for the Benjaminite warriors. This is still not enough so they devise the kidnapping of the girls of Shiloh – God's sanctuary – which enables the other two hundred men to have wives.

It is often considered heretical to believe that words of the Bible are not factually true but wholly fictional or legendary based on some seeds of historical truth. Would it not be better to believe that these were gross exaggerations to teach a moral lesson? Could any religious person today believe that any of our precursors were acting according to God's will, when for the sake of honour or to avoid breaking an oath they committed genocide? This is not to say that our ancestors did not believe that they were doing God's will. We need only consider the modern barbarism done in the name of God.

Why are these tales then included in the holy canon? The last verse of the book reveals it all – a verse which appears scattered throughout the **Book of Judges**, each man or tribe did what they pleased, and this is why the Israelites needed a king to impose order on them. Though biblical theology calls upon the Israelites to worship and obey God as their only king, a divine compromise is required. God must climb down from being sole ruler because he does not have the power to win the obedience of his people. The next historical biblical book, *Samuel*, shows how this transition is painfully achieved when Saul is appointed king.

Appendix

Appendix to Joshua

CHAPTER 12 · The conquered lands

These are the territorial kings whom the Israelites defeated, whose territories they took possession of: East of Jordan from the Wadi Arnon to Mount Hermon and the eastern part of Arabah, **the land of** King Sihon of the Amorites who lived in Heshbon and reigned over half of the Gilead, from Aroer which is on the border of the Wadi Arnon, up to the Wadi Jabbok on the border of the Ammonites, the Arabah up to the sea of Chinnereth on the east and up to the sea of the Arabah – The Dead Sea – on the east in the direction of Beth-jeshimoth and on the south to the slopes of Pisgah, the territories of King Og of Bashan, the last of the Rephaim, **the giants who were sired by women to the sons of the gods in ancient times** who lived in Ashtaroth and Edrei and ruled over Mount Hermon and Salcah and over all of Bashan up to the border of the Geshurites and Maacathites and half of the territory of Gilead up to the very border **of the land** under the rule of King Sihon of Heshbon. Moses, the servant of the LORD, and the Israelites defeated them. Moses, the servant of the LORD, gave these lands for a possession to the Reubenites, the Gadites and half of the tribe of Menasseh.

These are the territorial kings whom Joshua and the people of Israel vanquished west of the Jordan, from Baal-gad in the valley of Lebanon up to Mount Halak on the way to Seir. Joshua granted it as an inheritance to the tribes of Israel: in the hill-country, in the lowlands, in the Arabah, in the slopes **of Pisgah**, in the wilderness and in the Negev (the south) – **the land of** the Hittites, the Amorites, the Canaanites, the Perizzites, the Hivites and the Jebusites. **These are now numerated one by one:** The king of Jericho, the king of Ai (which is next to Bethel), the king of Hebron, the king of Jarmuth, the king of Lachish, the king of Eglon, the king of Gezer, the king of Debir, the king of Geder, the king of Hormah, the king of Arad, the king of Libnah, the king of Adullam, the king of Makkedah, the king of Beth-el, the king of Tappuah, the king of Hepher, the king of Aphek, the king of Sharon, the king of Madon, the king of Hazor, the king of Shim-ron-meron, the king of Achshaph, the king of Taanach, the king of Megiddo, the king of Kedesh, the king of Jokneam in Carmel, the king of Dor in the region of Dor, the king of Goiim in Gilgal, the king of Tirzah, all in all, thirty-one kings.

CHAPTERS 13 & 14 · The unconquered Lands

Now Joshua was old and advanced in years. The LORD said to him, "You are old and well- advanced in years and there yet remains much land to be conquered. These are the lands that remain to be captured: all the territories of the Philistines and the Geshurites, from Shihor, which is before Egypt up to the border of Ekron in the north which is considered as part of Canaan **and so promised by God to Abraham;** namely, the five lords of the Philistine city-states: Gaza, Ashdod, Ashkelon, Gath and Ekron, also the land of the Avvim, **Canaanites,** who lived on the south, all the land of the Canaanites from Mearah which is possessed by the Sidonians up to Aphek reaching the borders of the Amorites; and the territory of the Gebalites and the whole **valley of** Lebanon towards the sun rising from Baal-gad by Mount Hermon up to the edge of Hamath, all the inhabitants of the hill-country from Lebanon up to Misrephoth on the west, that is to say, all the Sidonians. I will **eventually** drive them out from before the people of Israel. Still, you may apportion these lands out to Israel to be their possession as I have commanded you. Now, therefore, divide the land as an inheritance for the nine tribes and half of the tribe of Manasseh."

Allocations made by Moses East of the Jordan
With the other half of the tribe of Menasseh, the Reubenites and the Gadites received their shares which Moses had allotted to

them east of the Jordan – as Moses the LORD's servant had indeed assigned to them: from Aroer on the edge of the Wadi Arnon and the city in the middle of the wadi, the entire tableland from Medeba to Dibon including all the towns of Sihon, king of the Amorites, who ruled from Heshbon unto the borders of the people of Ammon, further on to Gilead the territory of the Geshurites and the Maacathites and all of Mount Hermon and the whole of Bashan up to Salcah – the entire Kingdom of Og in Bashan who ruled both in Ashtaroth and in Edrei. He, **Og**, was the last of the Rephaim, **the giants of old who were descendants from the sons of God**[1] – for these did Moses defeat and dispossess. Still, the people of Israel did not dispossess the Geshurites nor the Maacathites. They live together with the Israelites even now. But to the tribe of Levi he gave no hereditary share of the land, their portion being the fire offerings of the LORD, the God of Israel, as he spoke concerning them to **Moses**.[2]

Allocations in greater detail
So Moses allocated **the following** to the clans of the tribe of the Reubenites: the territory from Aroer on the edge of the Wadi Arnon and the town in the middle of the wadi and all the tableland up to Medeba – including Heshbon and all the towns of the tableland: Dibon, Bamoth-baal, Beth-baal-meon, Jahaz, Kedemoth, Mephaath, Kiriathaim, Sibmah, Zereth-shahar in the hill of the valley, Beth-peor, the slopes of Pisgah, Beth-jeshimoth – all the towns of the tableland and the whole kingdom of Sihon, king of the Amorites, who had reigned in Heshbon, whom Moses defeated with the chiefs of Midian, Evi, Rekem, Zur, Hur and Riba – the princes of Sihon who dwelt in the territory. Together with

---

[1] There is a rabbinic tradition that Og was the last of the demigods – the **Anakim** – who rode out the flood by hitching himself to Noah's ark.
[2] The Levites, from whom the priests (**Cohanim**) came, benefited from the taxes accruing from the sacrificial rites.

the rest of those slain, the people of Israel put to the sword Balaam ben Beor the soothsayer.[1] The border of the territory of the Reubenites was the River Jordan. So this was the extent of the territory possessed by the clans of the Reubenites – including the towns and the villages surrounding them.

Moses allocated to the tribe of Gad portions for each of its clans. Their territory was Jazer, all the towns of Gilead and half of the territory of Ammon up to Aroer which is facing Rabbah; and from Heshbon until Ramath-mizpeh, and Betonim; from Mahanaim until the border of Lidbir; and in the Valley – Beth-haran and Beth-nimrah, Sukkoth and Zaphon and the rest of the kingdom of Sihon, the king of Heshbon, of which the border is the Jordan up until the tip of the sea of Chinnereth (also known as Gennasereth) on the east side of the Jordan. This was the territory given to the Gadites, for their clans **to be their possession** as a continual inheritance – those towns and villages.

Moses allocated land to the half-tribe of Manasseh for all its clans which became their territory. Their border extended from Mahanaim taking in all of the Bashan, all of the kingdom of Og, king of Bashan and all of the tent settlements of Jair which are in Bashan – sixty villages; half of Gilead and Ashtaroth and Edrei, the capitals of the kingdom of Og in Bashan – these were allocated to the descendants of Machir, the **only** son of Manasseh, for half of his descendants for their clans.

These are the allocations which Moses distributed in the Plains of Moab on the east side of the Jordan, near Jericho. To the tribe of Levi, Moses allocated no territory because the LORD, the God of Israel is their portion as the LORD had commanded concerning them.

---

[1] Balaam was paid by King Balak to curse the Israelites. On his way to his mission a Messenger of God gets in the way of the donkey who is carrying him. When the donkey halts, he beats it. After the third such beating, the donkey speaks in protest. God allows Balaam to prophesy but on the condition that he blesses the Israelites instead of cursing them. King Balak is outraged. This story is in the Book of Numbers.

Allocation in Canaan according to lots

These are the territories which the Israelites took as a permanent inheritance in the land of Canaan which were allocated to them under the supervision of Eleazar the priest and Joshua bin Nun and the heads of the patriarchal families of the tribes of Israel. It was done by lots as the LORD had instructed Moses regarding the distribution of territories for the nine and a half tribes. Moses had already allocated territories to be the inheritance of two and a half tribes on the other side of the Jordan, but to the Levites he gave no territory to be their inheritance. The sons of Joseph had become two tribes, Ephraim and Manasseh, **because Jacob had blessed Joseph with two portions of the land of Canaan, therefore the land was divided in twelve parts,** because no portion of the land was given to the tribe of Levi, except for villages to live in with open land about them for their cattle and livestock. The Israelites divided the land as the LORD had instructed Moses.

The claim of Caleb Ben Jephunneh

The elders of the tribe of Judah approached Joshua in Gilgal **in** support **of the claims** of Caleb ben Jephunneh, the Kenizzite, **who had married into the tribe of Judah** who said, "You know what the LORD said concerning me and you to Moses in Kadesh-barnea. I was forty years old when Moses, the servant of the LORD sent me from Kadesh-barnea to spy out the land and I brought him back my report **of what** I found according to my own views **and was not influenced by the other spies.**[1] Nevertheless, my brothers who had gone up with me made the heart of the people turn to

---

[1] Moses had sent out twelve spies to reconnoitre the land of Canaan. Ten spies reported that the land was unconquerable as the men were giants. Only Joshua and Caleb were positive about their ability to take possession of Canaan, see Numbers 14:1 ff; Deuteronomy 1:28. The punishment for Israel's cowardice and lack of faith was that all who left Egypt would wander in the wilderness for a further thirty-eight years until a new generation would emerge to conquer the land of Canaan. All the adults would die except for Caleb and Joshua.

jelly, but I believed entirely in the LORD, **that he would deliver our enemies into our hands.** On that day did Moses swear, 'The land on which your feet have trodden shall be your possession and that of your descendants for ever for you had total trust in the LORD, my God'.

"Now the LORD has kept me alive as he promised these forty-five years since the LORD made this promise **on my behalf** to Moses when the Israelites were yet in the wilderness. I am now eighty-five years old, but I am still as strong today as I was on the day that Moses sent me. As was my strength then, so is it now – to go into battle **and to do all that is required of a man.** Now, therefore, apportion to me this hill country **where Hebron is** of which the LORD spoke on that day because you heard them say then how the Anakim – giants – lived there and that the cities were of enormous size and well fortified. Perhaps the LORD will be with me, **according to his promise** and I will succeed to drive them out as the LORD has promised."

Joshua gave him his blessing. He allocated Hebron to Caleb ben Jephunneh to be his inheritance. So Hebron **eventually** became the possession of Caleb ben Jephunneh the Kennizzite until this very day because he fully trusted in the LORD, the God of Israel. The name of Hebron used to be Kiriath-arba (the town of Arba) for Arba was the greatest among the Anakim. And war ceased in the land because **the Israelites could conquer no more.**

CHAPTER 15 · The Land of Judah

The lot designating the territory of Judah for all its clans lay farthest south down to the border of Edom – the wilderness of Zin. Their southern border was from the tip of the Salt Sea from its tongue which looks towards the south. It extended south of the Scorpions' Pass which passes along to Zin and then to the south of Kadesh-barnea up to Hezron and Addar where it turns to Karka; then on to Azmon up to the wadi of Egypt. The end of the southern border was the Great Sea (Mediterranean). **This was**

Judah's southern border. The eastern border was the Salt Sea up to the mouth of the Jordan. The border ascended to Beth-hoglah passing north of Beth-arabah. The border extended as far as the Stone of Bohan, the descendant of Reuben. The border went up to Debir from the valley of Achor and further north facing Gilgal, over against the Ascent of Blood which is on the south side of the wadi. The border then stretches to the waters of En-shemesh (Spring of the Sun) and then on to En-rogel (the Fuller's Spring). The border extended along Gehinnom (The Valley of the Son of Hinnom) up to the southern side of the city of the Jebusites – that is Jerusalem – up to the top of the hills that lie before Gehinnom on the west which is at the northern extreme of the Vale of Rephaim. The border inclined from the top of the hill to the fountain of waters at Neftoah going to the towns of Mount Ephron. The border inclined to Baalah – that is Kiriath-jearim. The border turned from Baalah westward to Mount Seir then northward along the slope of Mount Jearim – that is Chesalon – going down to Beth-shemesh and on to Timnah. The border then extended to the northern side of Ekron. The border then inclined to Shikkeron, passing on to Mount Baalah proceeding to Jabneel. The borders extended to the Sea. The western border was the Great Sea. These were the boundaries of the clans of the people of Judah.

According to the LORD's instructions to Joshua, he gave a portion to Caleb ben Jephunneh among the people of Judah – that is Kiryath-arba (Arba was the ancestor of Anak) which is also called Hebron. Caleb disinherited the three sons of Anak: Sheshai, Ahiman and Talma **from their possession of Hebron. After this conquest,** he went on to attack the inhabitants of Debir which used to be called Kiriath-sepher. Caleb declared, "He who defeats Kiriath-sepher and conquers it, to him will I give Achsah, my daughter, to be his wife." Athniel ben Kinaz, the kinsman of Caleb, conquered it. So he gave him Achsah his daughter to be his wife.

When she became his wife, he induced her to ask her father

for a certain field. **When she came to her father** and dismounted from her donkey, Caleb asked her, "What do you want?" She replied, "Give me a blessing[1], for you have given me away as dry land, **empty handed, with no dowry,** so give me springs of water." So he gave her the upper and lower springs.

This was the territory of the clans of the tribes of Judah. The towns at the far end of Judah toward the border of Edom on the south were Kabzeel, Eder and Jagur; Kinah, Dimona and Adadah; Kedesh, Hazor and Ithnan; Ziph, Telem and Bealoth; Hazor; Hadattah and Kerioth; Hezron which is Hazor; Amam, Shema and Moladah; Hazar-gaddah, Heshmon and Beth-pelet; Hazar-shaul, Beer-sheba and Biziothials; Baalah, Iim and Ezem; Eltolad, Chesil and Hormah; Ziklag, Madmannah and Sansannah; Lebaoth, Shilhim, Ain and Rimmon – twenty-nine towns and their villages.

In the lowland: Eshtaol, Zorah and Ashnah; Zanoah, Engannim, Tapuah and Enam; Jarmuth, Adullam, Socoh and Azekah; Shaaraim, Adithaim, Gederah and Gederothaim – fourteen towns with their villages. Zenan, Hadashah and Migdal-gad; Dilan, Mizpeh and Joktheel; Lachish, Bozkath and Eglon; Cabbon, Lahmas and Chithlish; Gederoth, Beth-dagon, Naamah and Makkedah – sixteen towns with their villages. Libnah, Ether and Ashan; Iphtah, Ashnah and Nezib; Keilah, Achzib and Mareshah – nine towns with their villages. Ekron with its surrounding villages and suburbs; from Ekron towards the sea – all the towns near Ashdod with their suburbs; Ashdod and its villages and suburbs; Gaza and its villages and suburbs up to the wadi of Egypt and the edge of the Great Sea; and in the hill country: Shamir, Jattir and Socoh; Dannah, Kiriath-sannah – that is Debir; Anab, Eshtemoh and Anim; Goshen, Holon and Giloh – eleven towns with their villages; Arab, Rumah and Eshan; Janum, Bethtappuah and Aphekah; Humtah, Kiriath-arba – that is Hebron –

---

[1] The Hebrew *B'racha* which could also be read with different vowels as *B'rayha* – Well of Water.

and Zior – nine towns with their villages. Maon, Carmel, Ziph and Juttah; Jezreel, Jokdeam and Zanoah; Kain, Gibeah and Timnah – ten towns with their villages. Halhul, Beth-zur, Gedor, Maarath, Beth-anoth and Eltekon – six towns and their villages. Kiriath-baal – that is Kiriath-jearim – and Rabbah – two towns with their villages. In the wilderness: Beth-arabah, Middin, Secacah, Nibshan, the Town of Salt and En-gedi – six towns with their villages. But the tribe of Judah could not dispossess the Jebusites who lived in Jerusalem, so the tribesmen of Judah live together with the Jebusites in Jerusalem even unto this day.

CHAPTER 16 · The territory of the tribes of Joseph

The portion that fell to the tribes Joseph extended from the Jordan at Jericho – from the waters of Jericho on the east. From Jericho it extended through the hill country as far as Beth-el; from there to Luz and passed on to the border of the Archites at Ataroth, descending westward to the border of the Japhelites to the border of Lower Beth-horon up to Gezer and ran on to the sea. So the tribes of Joseph – Manasseh and Ephraim – received their promised inheritance.

The border of the Ephraimites, by their clans was as follows: the border of their inheritance extended from Atroth-addar on the east up to Upper Beth-horon. The border extended to the sea westward. On the north, the border extended from Michmethath to the east of Taanath-shiloh and passed beyond it to the east of Janoah. From Janoah it extended to Ataroth and Naarah until it reached Jericho and up to the Jordan. From Tappuah, the border extended westward to Wadi Kanah and up to the Sea. This is the inheritance of the tribe of Ephraim, according to their clans together with the towns allocated to the Ephraimites which were in the territory of the tribe of Manasseh – all the towns with their villages. But they could not drive out the Canaanites who lived in Gezer. The Canaanites lived within the territory of Ephraim even until now, but became forced labourers.

CHAPTER 17 · Manasseh's portion

This is the portion that fell by lot to the tribe of Manasseh – for he was Joseph's first-born. As for Machir, the first-born of Manasseh, the ancestor of the Gileadites, because they were great warriors, they were able to conquer the lands of Gilead and Bashan. Other allocations were made to the other clans, the descendants of Abiezer, Helek, Asriel, Shechem, Hepher and Shemida. These were the sons of Manasseh the son of Joseph, clan by clan.

But Zelophehad, the son of Hepher, the son of Gilead, the son of Machir, the son of Manasseh had no sons – only daughters whose names were Mahlah, Noah, Hoglah, Milcah and Tirzah. They approached Eleazar the priest and Joshua bin Nun and the chieftains. They said, "The LORD instructed Moses to give us an inheritance among our male kinsmen." So, as the LORD had instructed this, he gave them a portion among their father's kinsmen. Ten parts fell to Manasseh in addition to the lands of Gilead and Bashan, which are across the Jordan. This is because the daughters of Manasseh had an inheritance along with his male descendants, and the land of Gilead belonged to the other sons of Manasseh.

The border of Manasseh extended from Asher to Michmethath which is by Shechem. The border extends to the right towards the settlements of En-tappuah, but the district of Tappuah belonged to Manasseh but Tappuah itself, which was on the border of the territtory of Manasseh, belonged to the Ephraimites. The border then descended to the Wadi Kanah south of the wadi, by the towns which belonged to the Ephraimites among the towns of Manasseh. The border of Manasseh was on the north side of the wadi and continued on to the Sea. What lay to the south belonged to the Ephraimites and what lay to the north belonged to the tribe of Manasseh. The Sea was its border. This territory shared a border with the territory of the tribe of Asher on the north and with that of the territory of the tribe of Issachar on the east.

Within the territories of Issachar and Asher, the tribe of Manasseh inhabited Beth-shean and its villages and Ibleam and its villages and the region of Dor and its villages and the region of En-dor and its villages, the region of Taanach and its villages and the region of Megiddo and its villages – all of the three regions. But, the people of Manasseh were not able to drive out the native inhabitants of those regions for the Canaanites were determined to remain in the land. In time, when the people of Israel became dominant, they taxed them but did not dispossess them.

The descendants of Joseph – **the leaders of the tribes of Ephraim and Manasseh** – complained to Joshua, "Why have you given us by lot only one portion with only one territory to be our inheritance, seeing that we are a numerous people whom the LORD has blessed with such numbers?"[1] Joshua replied to them contemptuously:

- "If you are such a powerful people, go up into the forest and clear an area for yourself in the land of the Perizzites and the Rephaim if the hill-country of Ephraim is too small for you."
- "True, the hill-country is not enough for us but all the Canaanites who live in the area of the valley have iron chariots – those who live in Beth-shean and its villages and those who live in the valley of Jezreel. **They will not allow us to clear the forest for our own settlements.**"
- "You are a numerous people with great power. Therefore, you will not only enjoy one allotment. The hill-country will be yours. Though it is forest land, you will clear it to its furthest out-reaches You will dispossess the Canaanites in spite of their iron chariots and in spite of their might."[2]

---

[1] Especially as Jacob had promised his son a double portion among his brothers – see Genesis.
[2] The complaint of the Joseph tribes and the dialogue with Joshua seems misplaced here. It should come earlier before the granting of the lands that they are ultimately to conquer from the native inhabitants.

CHAPTER 18 · The meeting at Shiloh

The whole Council of the people of Israel assembled together at Shiloh and established a Tent of Meeting there. By that time **most of** the land had been conquered by them. But there remained seven tribes which had not yet received their **promised** allotment. Joshua reprimanded the leaders of Israel, "How long will you put off taking possession of the land of your inheritance which the LORD, the God of your ancestors has promised you? Appoint three men from every tribe. I will send them out to go throughout the country to do a survey, writing a description of the land according to their desired allocation – then let them bring it to me. They will divide the land in seven parts. Judah shall live within its borders in the south and the house of Joseph shall live within its borders in the north. When you have done surveys of the land divided into seven parts – bring the surveys to me. Then will I cast lots **to determine who will receive what** before the LORD. But, remember that the Levites will have no portion among you, for the priesthood of the LORD is their **promised and privileged** inheritance; also the tribes of Gad and Reuben and the half-tribe of Manasseh have received their allotment east of the Jordan, which Moses, the servant of the LORD gave them."

The men **who were appointed** proceeded to go and Joshua charged those who went to survey the land, "Go, travel throughout the land, survey it and return to me and then I will cast lots for you here before the LORD in Shiloh." So did the men go and travel throughout the land and recorded surveys of all the towns divided into seven sections in a scroll. They returned to Joshua at Shiloh. Joshua cast lots for them in Shiloh before the LORD and divided the land to the **seven** tribes of Israel according to their allotted divisions.

The first lot fell to the tribe of Benjamin and all their clans. The part allotted to them lay between the land of the tribe of Judah and the land of the tribes of Joseph. Their border on the north side began at the Jordan and ascended to the northern side of Jericho, going up through the hill-country towards the west extending into the wilderness of Beth-aven. From there the border extended southward to Luz, to the side of Luz which is Beth-el. From there the border extended down to Atroth-addar by the hill that lies south of Lower Beth-Horon. The border now inclined and turned on its western boundary. It continued southward from the hill on the south side of Beth-horon, extending to Kiriath-baal – that is Kiriath-jearim, a town belonging to the tribe of Judah. This was its western border. The southern border – from the edges of Kiriath-jearim the border extended eastward and extended to the fountains of the Waters of Nephtoah. Then the border descended to the lowest part of the hill that lies before the Valley of Ben-hinnom at the northern edge of the Valley of Rephaim. Then it went down to the Valley of Hinnom along the southern flank of Jebusite dwellings to En-rogel. Inclining northwards, it extended to En-shemesh and Geliloth which is facing the Ascent of Adummim, and descended to the Stone of Bohan ben Reuben. It continued northward to the edge of the Arabah and descended into the Arabah. The border passed on the northern side of Beth-hoglah. It finished at the northern tongue of the Salt Sea at the southern end of the Jordan. This was its southern border. The Jordan was also their border on the east. That was to be the allotment of the Benjaminites, all their clans – in accordance to the aforementioned borders on all sides.

The towns of the tribe of Benjamin, by its clans, were Jericho, Beth-hoglah and Emek-keziz; Beth-arabah, Zemarim and Beth-el; Avim, Parah and Ophrah; Chepher-ammonah, Ophni and Geba – twelve towns with their villages. Gibeon, Ramah and Beeroth, Mizpeh, Chephira and Mozah; Rekem, Irpeel and Taralah; Zela, Eleph and the town of the Jebusites – that is Jerusalem; Gibeath and Kiriath – fourteen towns with their villages. This is the promised allotment of the Benjaminites, by their clans.

CHAPTER 19 · Simeon's allocation

The second lot fell to Simeon – for the tribe of Simeon, by their clans. This part was inside the inheritance of the tribe of Judah. They had for their inheritance Beer-sheba [Sheba], Moladah, Hazor-shual, Balah and Ezem; Eltolad, Bethul and Hormah; Ziklag, Beth-marcaboth and Hazar-susah; Beth-lebaoth and Sharuhen – thirteen towns with their villages. Ain, Rimmon, Ether and Ashan – four towns with their villages. All the villages that surrounded these towns to Baalath-beer as far as Ramah of the South. This is the inheritance of the Simeonites by their clans. The portion of the Simeonites was part of the territory of the tribe of Judah for it had more than it needed. Therefore, the Simeonites had their portion among them.

The third lot fell to the tribe of Zebulun, by their clans and the borders of their innheritance: starting at Sarid, their **southern** border went westward up to Maralah touchinng Dabbesheth and the wadi that is by Jokneam. From Sarid along the eastern side where the sun rises past the border of Chisloth-tabor, on to Dobrath and up to Japhia. From there it moved eastward to Gath-hepher, to Eth-kazim, on to Rimmon-methnoar where it inclined to Neah. Then it turned – that is its northern border to Hannathon. Its north-west limit was at the Valley of Iphtah-el, Kattath, Nahalal, Shimron, Idalah and Beth-lehem (of Galilee) – twelve towns with their villages. This is the portion of the Zebulunites, by their clans – these towns with their villages.

The fourth lot fell to Issachar, by their clans. Their territory included Jezreel, Chesulloth and Shunem; Hapharaim, Shion and Anaharath; Rabbith, Kishion and Ebez; Remeth, En-gannim, En-haddah and Beth-pazzez. The border reached Tabor, Shashazim and Beth-shemesh. Their border reached the Jordan – sixteen towns with their villages. This is the portion of the tribe of Issacharites, by their clans – the towns with their villages.

The fifth lot fell to the tribe of Asher, by their clans. Their territory included Helkath, Hali, Beten and Achshaph, Allammelech, Amad and Mishal. It reached Carmel on the west and to Shihor-libnath. It turned **from Helkath** along the east side to Beth-dagon touching the territory of Zebulun and the Valley of Iphtah-el on the north, Beth-emek and Neiel. It reached Cabul on its northern side; Ebron, Rehob, Hammon, Kanah up to Great Sidon. The border then turned to Ramah and to the fortified city of Tyre. Then the border turned to Hosah and its limits to the west were from Hebel to Achzib; Ummah, Aphek and Rehob – twenty-two towns with their villages. This is the allotment of the tribe of the Asherites by their clans – these towns with their villages.

The sixth lot fell to the tribe of Naphtali, for the Naphtalites, by their clans. Their border started at Heleph, Elon-bezaanannim, Adami-nekeb and Jabneel to Lakum and it ended at the Jordan. The border then turned westward to Aznoth-tabor and from there to Hukok. It touched the territory of Zebulun on the south. It touched Asher on the west and Judah at the Jordan on the east. The fortified towns were Ziddim-zer, Hammath, Rakkath and Chinnereth; Adamah, Ramah and Hazor; Kedesh, Edre and En-hazor; Iron, Migdal-el, Horem, Beth-anath and Beth-shemesh – nineteen towns with their villages. This is the allotment of the tribe of the Naphtalites, by their clans – these towns with their villages.

The seventh lot fell to the tribe of the Danites, by their clans. Their allotted territory included Zorah, Eshtaol and Ir-shemesh; Shaal-abbin, Aijalon and Ithlah; Elon, Timnah and Ekron, Elte-keh, Gibbethon and Baalath; Jehud, Bene-berak and Gath-rimmon; Me-jarkon and Rakkon with the border facing Joppa. But when the Danites could not hold on to their territories, they fought against the people of Leshem (Laish)[1]. They conquered it by the sword and possessed it. They lived there and called Leshem Dan after Dan their ancestral patriarch. This is the **promised**

---

[1] See Judges p. 86ff for the gory details.

allotment of the Danites, by their clans – these towns with their villages.

When they had finished allocating the land according to these borders, the Israelites gave a portion in their midst to Joshua bin Nun. This was in accordance with the instructions of the LORD. They gave him the town for which he asked – Timnath-serah in the hill-country of Ephraim. He fortified the town and lived there.

These are the portions which Eleazar the priest and Joshua bin Nun and the heads of the ancestral houses assigned by lot to the tribes of Israel at the entrance of the Tent of Meeting. So they completed the task of dividing up the land.

CHAPTER 20 · Cities of refuge

The LORD instructed Joshua, "Say this to the people of Israel, 'Establish towns for refuge as I instructed you through Moses – so that a man who kills a person by error or unintentionally may run there **for refuge** from the blood avengers.[1] He will run to one of these towns, stand by the gate of the town and make his case before the town's elders. They shall admit him into their town and give him a place so that he may live among them. If the blood avenger pursues him, they must not hand the fugitive over to him, because he unintentionally killed his neighbour and was not motivated by any previous hatred. He shall live in that town until he stands trial before the community **and remain there** until the death of the High Priest who is in office at that time. Then the fugitive may return to his own town and home from where he fled'."

As towns of refuge, they designated Kedesh in the hill-country of Naphtali in Galilee; Shechem in the hill-country of Ephraim

---

[1] It was the 'moral' duty of the next of kin to avenge the blood even against an innocent perpetrator or more likely one who had committed man-slaughter.
The towns of refuge provided an option not only for the 'killer' but for the next of kin of the murdered to avoid a cycle of death between the families of the victim and his murderer.

and Kiriath-arba – that is Hebron – in the hill-country of Judah. Across the Jordan, east of Jericho, they designated Bezer in the wilderness, in the Tableland, from the tribe of Reuben; Ramoth in Gilead from the tribe of Gad and Golan in Bashan from the tribe of Manasseh. These were the designated towns for all the people of Israel and even for the resident aliens – that anyone who kills someone unintentionally might take refuge there and not die by the hand of the blood avenger before standing trial before the community.

CHAPTER 20 · The portion of the Levites

The heads of the ancestral houses of the Levites came to Eleazar the priest and Joshua bin Nun and to the heads of the ancestral houses of the tribes of Israel. They made this plea at Shiloh in the land of Canaan, "Through Moses the LORD instructed that we be given towns to dwell in with pastures for our livestock." So the tribes of Israel gave towns and pastures to the Levites from their own allotment as the LORD had instructed – these towns with their pastures.

The **first** lot among the Levites fell to the Kohathite clans. To the descendants of Aaron the priest, there fell by lot thirteen towns from the tribes of Judah, Simeon and Benjamin. To the remaining Kohathites there fell by lot ten towns from the clans of the tribes of Ephraim; from the tribe of Dan and from the half-tribe of Manasseh.

To the Gershonites, there fell by lot thirteen towns from the clans of the tribes of Issachar, Asher, Naphtali and the half-tribe of Manasseh in Bashan. To the Merarites, by their clans – twelve towns from the tribes of Reuben, Gad and Zebulun. The people of Israel gave by lot these towns with their pasture land to the Levites as the LORD had instructed through Moses.

From the tribes of Judah and Simeon there were the assigned towns listed by names. They were for the descendants of Aaron among the Kohathite clans of the Levites. The first lot fell to them:

To them were given Kiriath-arba (Arba was the father of Anak) – that is Hebron – which is in the hill country of Judah with the pasture land around it. But the fields of the city with its villages they gave to Caleb ben Jephunnah to be his possession. But to the descendants of Aaron the priest they assigned Hebron – (the town of refuge for the unintentional killer) – and its pastures and Libnah with its pastures; also Jattir and Eshtemoa with its pastures; Holon and Debir with their pastures; Ain, Juttah, Beth-shemesh with their pastures – nine towns from those two tribes. From the tribe of Benjamin, Gibeon and Geba with their pastures; Anathoth and Almon with their pastures – four towns. All the towns with their pastures assigned to the descendants of Aaron the priest numbered thirteen.

As regards the clans of the Kohathites, those remaining Levites descended from Kohath, the towns that fell to them by lot were from the tribe of Ephraim. They gave them Shechem with her pastures in the hill-country of Ephraim (the town of refuge for the unintentional killer) and Gezer with her pastures; Kibzaim and Beth-horon with their pastures – four towns. From the tribe of Dan, Elteke, Gibbethon and their pastures; Aijalon, Gath-rimmon with their pastures – four towns. From the half-tribe of Manasseh, Taanach and Gath-rimmon with their pastures – two towns. All the towns and their pasture land for the remaining clans of the Kohathites were ten.

To the descendants of Gershon from the clans of the Levites, the half-tribe of Manasseh gave Golan with her pastures in Bashan (a town of refuge for the unintentional killer) and Beeshterah with her pastures – two towns. From the tribe of Issachar, Kishion and Dobrath with their pastures; Jarmuth and En-gannim with their pastures – four towns. From the tribe of Asher, Mishal and Abdon with their pastures; Helkath and Rehob with their pastures – four towns. From the tribe of Naphtali, Kedesh in Galilee (a town of refuge for the unintentional killer) and Hammoth-dor and Kartan with their pastures – three towns. All the towns and their pasture land for the Gershonite by their clans were thirteen.

In regard to the remaining Levites, the clans of the Merarites: From the tribe of Zebulun, Jokneam and Karath with their pastures; Dimnah and Nahalal with their pastures – four towns. From the tribe of Gad, Ramoth in Gilead (a town of refuge for the unintentional killer) and Mahanaim with their pastures; Heshbon and Jazer with their pastures – four towns in all. All these were the towns of the Merarites, by their clans – the remaining Levitical clans – numbering twelve.

All the towns of the Levites – forty-eight towns with their pasture lands – were within the portions of the other Israelite tribes. Thus were those towns assigned, each with its surrounding pastures. So it was with every town.

Thus did the LORD grant unto Israel all the land which he had sworn to give to their fathers. They took possession of it and lived in it. The LORD gave them rest on all fronts as he had sworn to their fathers. Not one man of all their enemies was able to withstand them. The LORD delivered all their enemies into their hand. Not one of the good things which the LORD had promised to the house of Israel was lacking. All were fulfilled.[1]

---

[1] Considering other parts of Joshua and Judges, this paragraph appears to be expressing more theological wish fulfilment based on the concept of an almighty God than the reality of Israel's tribal history.

Appendix to Judges

CHAPTER 1

After Joshua's death, the people of Israel asked the LORD: "Who should first do battle on our behalf against the Canaanites?" The LORD answered, "Judah shall go up to do battle. See I have given the land into his hand." The leaders of Judah said to their colleagues of the tribe of Simeon, "Join me in going into my allotted territory to fight the Canaanites, and we will reciprocate by fighting for your share." The Simeonites agreed and went up with them. So when the warriors of Judah went out to battle, the LORD delivered the Canaanites and Perizzites into their hands. They killed ten thousand men in Bezek. They found King Adoni-bezek in Bezek where they attacked him when they defeated the Canaanites and Perizzites. But Adoni-bezek fled. They caught up with him and cut off his thumbs and great toes. Adoni-zedek said,

"The thumbs and great toes of seventy kings,
Had I cut off.
They scrounged for crumbs under my table.
As I have done,
So God has done to me."

They took him to Jerusalem where he died.

The men of Judah fought against Jerusalem, captured it by the sword and burnt it down.[1] After this the men of Judah went out to attack the Canaanites that lived in the hill-country, in the Negev [the south] and in the lowlands. Judah then attacked the

[1] This is an incredible claim as thirteen verses later in this chapter 1:21, we are informed that the Benjaminites could not conquer it. In Joshua 15:63 we are informed that the tribe of Judah could not drive them out (the Jebusites of Jerusalem). The Amarna letters record that King Abdi-hupa of Jerusalem remained loyal to the Pharaoh Akhenaton (1375–1358 BCE) while the rest of the country was being overrun by the Haberus (Hebrews). How the editor of Joshua and Judges could have allowed this blatant contradiction is a complete mystery.

Canaanites who lived in Hebron, which used to be called Kiriath-arba, where they defended its lords: Sheshai, Ahimon and Talmai. From there they attacked the inhabitants of Debir, which used to be called Kiriath-sepher.

Caleb, **an elder of Judah who with Joshua was the only Israelite who left Egypt and survived to enter Canaan**[1], said, "He who leads to the capture of Kiriath-sepher will have Achsah my daughter to be his wife." Othniel, the son of Kenaz, Caleb's younger kinsman, captured it, so he gave his daughter Achsah to him to be his wife. When she came to him **from Hebron**, she persuaded him to **give her permission to** ask her father for a certain field. When she got off her donkey, Caleb asked her, "What do you want from me?" "Give me a blessing for **by marrying me to Othniel** you have made me live in the southlands. Give me, therefore, springs of water[2], **so that during the dry seasons we will not lack water.**" So Caleb gave her the field containing the Gulloth-illith and the Gulloth-tachlith [the upper and lower springs in a valley near Hebron].

The descendants of the Kenite who was Moses' father-in-law left the City of Palm Trees with the men of Judah to go into the wilderness of Judah and settled there among the Amalekites to the south of Arad. Judah went with Simeon, his brother tribe, and they struck down the Canaanites that lived in Zepath. They wiped it out so that the town was called Hormah (Wipe-out). But Judah could not capture Gaza nor Ashkelon,[3] nor Ekron and the

---

[1] More about Caleb can be found in the Appendix to Joshua, see p. 107ff.
[2] It is of etymological interest that the Hebrew root for blessing, b-r-ch is the same for the Hebrew words: water spring' and 'knee.' One bent the knee to drink water from a spring. In ancient days water was the source of all economic blessings. It may be the reason we bend our knees in prayer – to thank God for his blessings; or the reason for bowing to any ruler.
[3] The Hebrew text says that Judah conquered Gaza but the ancient Greek translation, the Septuagint, says that Judah could *not* conquer the Philistine cities. In view of the later historical narratives, the Septuagint appears to be the correct version.

territories under their control. The LORD was, however, with Judah so that he drove out those who lived in the hill-country, but he could not drive out those who lived in the plain for they possessed iron chariots. They gave Hebron to Caleb according to the instructions of Moses, from where he drove out the three sons of Anak. The Benjaminites could not drive out the Jebusites who lived in Jerusalem, so that the Jebusites live with the Benjaminites in Jerusalem to this very day.

The house of Joseph – they advanced against Beth-el and the LORD was with them. When the house of Joseph sent out scouts to Beth-el – whose former name was Luz – they saw a man coming out of the town. They said to him, "Please show us how to enter the town and we will reward you generously." He told them how to enter the town. So they were able to strike the city down by the force of the sword. But they allowed their informant and his family to leave unharmed. That man went into the country of the Hittites. There he built a town which he named Luz, **after the town he had betrayed and forsaken**, which is still its name today.

But Manasseh was not able to disinherit the inhabitants of Beth-shean, nor of Taanach, nor of Dor, nor Ibleam, nor of Megiddo and all their villages because the Canaanites were determined to hold on to their land. Eventually, when the Israelites became dominant, they imposed forced labour upon them but they never dispossessed them. Equally, Ephraim did not expel the Canaanites who lived in Gezer but the Canaanites lived in Gezer among them. Zebulun did not disinherit the inhabitants of Kitron or Nahalol – the Canaanites lived among them but were subject to taxes.

Asher could not dispossess the inhabitants of Acco, nor of Sidon, nor of Ahlab, nor of Achzib, nor of Helbah, nor of Aphik, nor of Rehob. The Asherites lived among the Canaanites who were the natives of the land, for they could not dispossess them. **Naphtali equally could not dispossess the inhabitants of Beth-shemesh and Beth-anath, but he lived among the Canaanites, the** natives of the land. But the natives were subjected to forced labour. As to the Danites, the Amorites forced them into the hill country. They did not allow them to come down to the plains. For the Amorites were determined to hold on to Har-heres, in Aijalon and in Shaalbim. Eventually, the House of Joseph became too strong for them and they were subjected to forced labour. The territory of the Amorites extended from the Ascent of Akrabbim; from Sela and onward.

CHAPTER 2:6–10 · Joshua's death recounted
When Joshua had dismissed the people, the Israelites – every on of them – went to their allotted portions and took possession of their territories. The people were obedient to the LORD all the days of Joshua's rule and all the days of the elders who outlived Joshua but who were witness to the great works the LORD had accomplished for Israel. Joshua bin Nun, the servant of the LORD, died at the age of a hundred and ten years. They buried him in the territory of his inheritance in Timnath-heres, in the hill-country of Ephraim on the north of Mount Gaash. All that generation were also soon gathered to their fathers. Another generation arose after them that did not know the LORD nor what he had done for Israel.

CHAPTER 2:20 – 3:6 · Why God did not keep the Covenant
The LORD was furious with Israel. He declared, "Because this nation has transgressed my covenant which I made with their fathers and has not obeyed me, I too **will not keep my part of the covenant and** will not dispossess the nations before them – those that Joshua did not conquer before he died. So by their presence, I may test Israel, whether they will keep the ways of the LORD to walk in them as did their fathers or not!" So the LORD left those nations intact without rushing to dispossess them, nor had he delivered them into the hand of Joshua.

Now these are the nations which the LORD left intact to test by them the Israelites who had not experienced all the wars in Canaan **which Joshua and the former generation had fought,** so that the next generations of Israelites might be taught to fight – but only those who had not experienced the former wars – the five regal cities of the Philistines and all the Canaanites and the Sidonians and the Hivites that lived in the hill-country of Lebanon from Mount Baal-hermon to Lebo-hamath. They were there **only** to prove the Israelites by their presence to know whether they would obey the LORD's commandments, which he commanded to their fathers through Moses **or whether they would follow the foreign gods of the natives.**[1] So the Israelites lived among the Canaanites, the Hittites, the Amorites, the Perizzites, the Hivites and the Jebusites. They took their daughters to be their wives and gave their own daughters to their sons and served their gods.

[1] The convoluted reasoning is that the natives were not dispossessed immediately so that God could reward or punish the new generation of Israelites who had not experienced his previous miraculous interventions. If they were loyal to him he would make the native populations subject to them. If they were not, the Israelites would be oppressed by them. Because of God's compassion, however, even when the Israelites are wicked, he will, when he is so moved, send them Judges – champion warriors to deliver them from their overlords.